ENERGY

25 Projects

Investigate

Why We Need Power & How We Get It

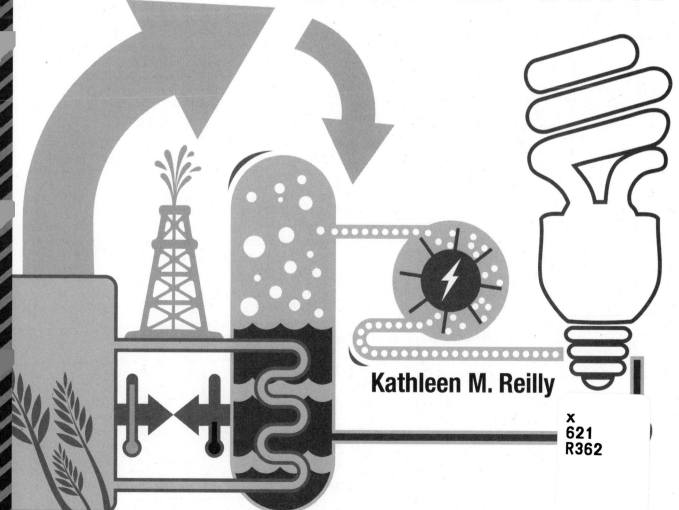

Kathleen M. Reilly

Questions regarding the ordering of this book should be addressed to
Independent Publishers Group
814 N. Franklin St.
Chicago, IL 60610
www.ipgbook.com

Nomad Press
2456 Christian St.
White River Junction, VT 05001

Other Titles in the Build It Series

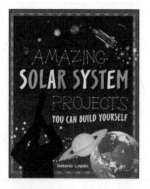

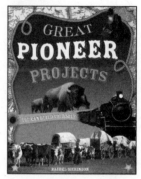

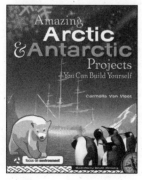

green
press
INITIATIVE

Nomad Press is committed to preserving ancient forests and natural resources. We elected to print *Energy: 25 Projects Investigate Why We Need Power & How We Get It* on 4,334 lb. of Rolland Enviro100 Print instead of virgin fibres paper. This reduces an ecological footprint of:

Tree(s): 37
Solid waste: 1,062kg
Water: 100,445L
Suspended particles in the water: 6.7kg
Air emissions: 2,332kg
Natural gas: 152m3

It's the equivalent of:
Tree(s): 0.8 American football field(s)
Water: a shower of 4.7 day(s)
Air emissions: emissions of 0.5 car(s) per year

Nomad Press made this paper choice because our printer, Transcontinental, is a member of Green Press Initiative, a nonprofit program dedicated to supporting authors, publishers, and suppliers in their efforts to reduce their use of fiber obtained from endangered forests.

For more information, visit www.greenpressinitiative.org

FSC

Recycled
Supporting responsible
use of forest resources

Cert no. SW-COC-000952
www.fsc.org
© 1996 Forest Stewardship Council

CONTENTS

Glossary ⚡ Resources ⚡ Index

Famous People In Energy

- **Isaac Newton** (1643–1727) explained the laws of motion and gravity—the forces that affect how work is done and energy is used.

- **Benjamin Franklin** (1706–1790) proved that lightning is really static electricity.

- **Michael Faraday** (1791–1867) explored electricity and magnetism. He invented the induction ring, which was the first electric transformer.

- **James Prescott Joule** (1818–1889) helped create the law of energy that states energy can't be destroyed. The international unit of energy (joule) is named after him.

- **Edwin Laurentine Drake** (1819–1880) was the first to drill for petroleum, essentially starting the oil industry.

- **Nicolaus August Otto** (1832–1891) invented the first gas engine (internal combustion engine). Up until this point, the world had been relying on a steam engine.

- **Karl Friedrich Benz** (1844–1929) invented the gasoline-powered automobile.

- **Thomas Edison** (1847–1931) realized it would be easy and efficient to light homes using electricity. He invented the light bulb and created the first power plant.

- **Lewis Howard Latimer** (1848–1928) perfected the light bulb by improving production of the carbon filaments that went into the bulbs.

- **Nikola Tesla** (1856–1943) made big advances in the fields of electricity and magnetism. He invented alternating electrical current (AC).

- **Rudolf Diesel** (1858–1913) created the combustion engine for use in very large machines. The engines are still named after him today.

- **Marie Curie** (1867–1934), along with her husband, discovered the first radioactive element, radium, by grinding up uranium ore.

- **Lise Meitner** (1878–1968) split the nucleus of uranium and called the process fission.

- **Albert Einstein** (1879–1955) experimented with energy and made tremendous advances in the field of physics.

- **Robert Goddard** (1882–1945) made advancements and developments in creating rockets.

- **J. Robert Oppenheimer** (1904–1967) is called the "father of the atomic bomb" because of his work in developing the first nuclear bomb.

Introduction

Energy Basics

You know what it feels like to have **energy**—you're up and on the go, and you feel like you just can't settle down. You probably also know what it feels like to run out of energy—like you could curl up and sleep all day, when even holding your head up feels like a chore.

Living things need energy to survive. In order to eat, move, play, think, attend school, catch a football, chat on the computer, and even to sleep, you need energy. In the wild, animals have to have energy to find food, escape predators, and capture prey.

What about non-living things? They need energy, too. Your car isn't going to get you to the beach without the energy to power it. You can't send an email without your computer being powered by energy. And your house won't be warm in the winter and cool in the summer without energy.

Words to Know

energy: the ability or power to do things, to work.

work: any kind of activity.

force: physical pressure that's applied to something.

electricity: energy made available by the flow of an electric charge through a conductor.

energy carrier: something that can transfer energy to something else, like a lamp. Something that moves energy in a usable form from one place to another.

While you hear about energy every day, needing energy isn't something that's new to humans. Ancient cave dwellers may not have been able to "tune in" and catch the nightly news on wide-screen televisions or call the local dinomart to order a pizza. But they still needed energy in the form of heat, to stay warm and to cook their food. So they burned wood.

All that makes sense, right? But what is energy? How does it work in so many different ways?

Simply put, energy is the ability to do **work**. Without energy, nothing would move, change, or grow. In this case, "work" doesn't specifically mean doing your homework or sweeping out the garage (although you do need energy to do those things!).

Scientists define work as when a **force** is applied to an object. A force is something that pushes or pulls on something else. That force transfers energy to the object, making the object move. Think about sweeping the garage again. You apply pressure to the broom, pushing and pulling on it. You're transferring your energy to the broom—and it's doing work for you. All over the world, from rabbits munching on grass to power plants generating **electricity**, work is being done. You may think energy is electricity. That's partly right. But electricity isn't a source of energy. It's an **energy carrier**. You'll explore that idea more later in this book.

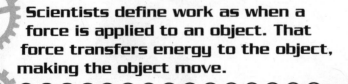

Scientists define work as when a force is applied to an object. That force transfers energy to the object, making the object move.

Coal, oil, the sun, and the wind are all sources of stored energy, much like the compressed spring or stretched rubber band. Humans transform those energy sources into electricity and other energy carriers that we can use to light our lamps and move our cars.

Energy sources are the things that have **stored energy**. A great example of stored energy is a wire spring. Imagine you have that small spring between your thumb and forefinger. When you squeeze down, you're applying a force on the spring. You know what will happen if you release your fingers—that spring will go flying. It has stored energy. When you do finally release it, the spring pushes back against your fingers, releasing that energy again and launching it-self. Same thing with a rubber band. You stretch it out nice and tight and it's loaded with stored energy.

When you release it—zing! Off it goes toward your target, changing that energy into motion.

In this book, you'll explore different sources of energy, along with electricity and **hydrogen**, which are carriers of energy. You'll discover the various ways that we use those energy sources, and what's beneficial (or not) about using them. And you'll be able to get hands-on with the different sources so you can see for yourself what all the energy buzz is about.

stored energy

3

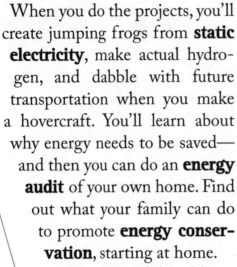

When you do the projects, you'll create jumping frogs from **static electricity**, make actual hydrogen, and dabble with future transportation when you make a hovercraft. You'll learn about why energy needs to be saved—and then you can do an **energy audit** of your own home. Find out what your family can do to promote **energy conservation**, starting at home.

You should be able to find most of the materials you'll need around your house. The materials you don't have should be pretty easy to get

static electricity: a build-up of an electric charge on an object (like you!)

energy audit: measuring how much energy is used and finding where it is being wasted.

energy conservation: decreasing energy use.

electrons: particles in atoms with a negative charge.

electric charge: when there is an imbalance of electrons, either too many or not enough.

at your local hardware store (and cheap, too!). Or, try getting them for free by asking for scraps from the hardware store or builders. Use recycled supplies whenever possible. That will save energy!

Go ahead and turn the pages to get started. You'll be using some stored energy inside your body to apply a force to each page to make it work for you—and you'll be glad you did!

Did you know?

Static electricity is worse in the winter because the air is dry. The air in the summer is more humid. The water in the summer air helps **electrons** move off you more quickly, so you do not build up an **electric charge.**

Chapter 1

What's the Buzz? What Energy Really Is

When you're really tired, you say you have no energy. When the cell phone dies and needs to be recharged, it's out of energy. But what is energy?

Energy is the ability to make things happen—to do work. It doesn't matter if it's a living creature or a school bus, everything needs energy to move and do things. Whether you're running a marathon or taking a nap, you're using energy to move, breathe, and make your body go. When a tree grows, it's using energy. And non-living things, like the hands on a clock, use energy to move, too.

DOES IT MATTER?

There's a saying, "Energy cannot be created or destroyed." That's because everything in the universe is made up of **matter**. Anything that takes up space and has **mass** is matter. An electric guitar is made of matter. An imaginary guitar is not. You're made of matter, and so is your cat, your best friend, your family minivan, and everything else you can physically touch in the entire world.

Even air is made out of matter. You may think that because you can't see or feel air, it must not have matter, but it does. Think of it this way: if you fill up a balloon with air, you can see the shape of the air filling it up. Air fills it because it's made of oxygen, nitrogen, and carbon dioxide **molecules**.

Atoms are the tiny particles that come together in certain ways and make up all matter.

Imagine you have a very strong microscope and put a piece of matter, like a bit of an apple, under it. If you zoomed in, you'd see the **cells** that make up the apple. Keep zooming in and you'd eventually see what matter is made up of—**atoms**. These are the microscopic parts that, when they come together in a particular way, make up everything.

Atoms are matter. They can't be created or destroyed. If you're thinking, "Whoa, if I eat that apple, I'm destroying it," you're partly right.

The apple was grown from a **chemical reaction** the sun's energy started, called **photosynthesis**. Then, you gobbled up the apple (using energy to eat it). The apple itself, a round, red piece of fruit, no longer exists in that form. You chewed it up and your stomach digested it. But the atoms that made up that apple are still around—they just got rearranged (teeth can do that) and used for other things. In this case, your body took what it needed from the apple to absorb into your body, using it as fuel to make you move and grow.

Think of it like this. An apple tree takes the sun's energy and converts it into sugars using photosynthesis. The sugars, called carbohydrates, give the tree the energy to grow apples. You eat the apple, and convert it into energy for your body to use. Your body might use it to run, or in "behind the scenes" ways, like building cells or maintaining your body heat. Energy changes forms, but it's still in the universe in some way. It never—poof!—disappears.

Without energy, living things couldn't move or grow. We wouldn't be able to use things like videogames or bicycles. Think about all the different things that move or do work. Now think about what would happen if we had no energy at all.

ENERGY OR POWER?

Sometimes we use the words "energy" and "power" to mean the same thing. They are similar, but there is a difference between them. You just saw that energy is the ability to do work. If something has an energy source, say, if your car has gasoline or if your MP3 player has charged batteries, it can do work. Your car can drive and your MP3 player can play music.

Power is the measurement of energy being used up over time. The more power something has, the more energy it uses.

There's another difference: Energy can't be created or destroyed. It changes forms, but it's always present in the universe. Power is created. You create power when you use energy. If you flip on a light switch to light a room for an hour, you're using power over a period of time. That usage can be measured—and that's power. When the light is off, there's no power.

But now that the words have been defined, here's the catch: Sometimes the words are used to mean the same thing! That's why "nuclear power" and "nuclear energy" mean the same thing—energy that's created from atoms. The words "energy" and "power" are partners.

Energy is the ability to do work. Power is energy used over time.

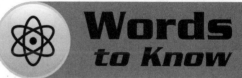

Words to Know

matter: the stuff that everything in the universe is made out of.

mass: a collection of particles.

molecule: a group of atoms bound together. Water is made of water molecules—H_2O—that are two hydrogen atoms bound to one oxygen atom.

cell: the small units of a living thing.

atom: the smallest particles that make everything.

chemical reaction: when atoms in a substance are rearranged to make a new substance.

substance: matter.

photosynthesis: the process of plants using water and the sun's energy to grow.

power: energy used over time.

ENERGY

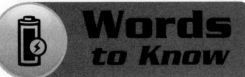

Words to Know

potential energy: stored energy.

gravity: the force of attraction that pulls all objects to the earth's surface.

kinetic energy: energy in motion.

mechanical energy: energy that uses physical parts you can see, like the parts of a machine.

chemical energy: energy produced by a chemical reaction.

TYPES OF ENERGY

If something's not moving or doing work, does it have energy? Yes, it has **potential energy**. That's when an object isn't in motion or doing work—but is in "suspended animation," waiting to be released. Think about a tiger stalking her prey. The tiger is frozen, tense, unmoving. She has potential energy stored in her muscles. Just like the tiger, a fresh battery in the drawer has potential energy, too.

If a ball is sitting on the ground, does it have energy? You may not think it does, but it has potential energy. That's because the force of **gravity** is working on the ball even as it sits there—holding it on the ground. Think about the tiger again, stalking. When the tiger launches into her strike, that energy explodes into motion. This is called **kinetic energy**. Kinetic energy is energy in motion.

Energy can be converted between potential and kinetic energy. If you pull a battery out of a drawer, pop it into a remote control car and start playing with the car, you're converting the battery's potential energy into the car's kinetic energy.

Because energy can be "handed off" between objects, it's never really destroyed—just transferred. That's called the "law of conservation of energy." Here's an example of this law: A tree grows using the energy it gets from the sun. It converts the sun's energy into sugars that it uses for food and to make more wood. After it has finished growing, the tree is cut down. The tree's energy is still inside the wood, stored as potential energy. Someone uses a log from that tree to make a campfire, and the tree's potential energy is converted into heat energy. That heat travels into our environment. The heat energy may warm you up, for example.

Did you know?

Some appliances—like television sets—use energy even when they're turned off! They're called phantom loads or energy vampires. Unplugging these energy vampires when you are not using them saves energy.

IT'S NOT ALL CREATED THE SAME

Mechanical energy results from potential or kinetic energy exerting a force on something with moving parts, like a windmill. The windmill can turn a stone that grinds corn. All those moving parts are creating mechanical energy.

In the chapter about electricity, you'll see that batteries work because of a chemical reaction that's going on inside them. That power is the result of **chemical energy**.

Energy can be converted between the different types. For example, our car burns gasoline to make it move. That's chemical energy being converted to mechanical energy.

But still—energy is being transferred. It is not being destroyed. Even when the fuel gauge on your car reads "empty," the gasoline is gone, but not the energy that it contained. That was transferred to mechanical energy to make your car move. When your car burns the gas, the energy is converted to heat energy (the engine gets hot!) and carbon dioxide and water vapor are released into the air. These gases contain potential energy.

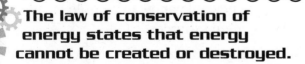

The law of conservation of energy states that energy cannot be created or destroyed.

9

KEEP IT GOING

solar power

Although energy can't be created or destroyed, the things that provide us with energy can be created or used up. This depends on whether the energy source is **renewable** or **non-renewable**. Think again about the gasoline that goes in a car. When the gasoline is burned, the energy itself continues on in other forms through heat or gases. But the actual liquid gasoline that you put in your car is gone forever.

Some sources of energy can keep replenishing themselves, like wood, solar power, or wind power. This is called renewable energy. But if there's a limit to the source, like oil, natural gas, and coal, then it's called non-renewable. Once that source is used up, we can't make more. So while the energy itself is continuing on in other forms, we can't harness that gasoline ever again to make our car go. If the car only runs on gasoline and the gasoline is gone, you won't have anything to put in your car.

wind power

WHERE DOES OUR ENERGY COME FROM?

Our energy sources include:

Petroleum: This non-renewable fossil fuel is used to heat our homes and fuel our cars. Also called oil and gasoline.

Natural Gas: Another non-renewable fossil fuel, natural gas is a common energy source for heat.

Coal: Coal is a non-renewable fossil fuel burned to generate electricity.

Nuclear: Harnessing the power of atoms makes nuclear power an important source of energy.

Wind: Moving air can provide generators with renewable energy to transform into electricity.

Hydropower: Renewable water power can generate electricity.

Solar: The sun's renewable energy can be captured to heat water or generate electricity.

Geothermal: The earth's heat is renewable and can be used as an energy source.

Biomass: Recently living things such as wood or manure are renewable sources of energy when burned.

FOSSIL FUELS

Fossil fuels are an important but non-renewable energy source. Oil, natural gas, and coal are all fossil fuels. Fossil fuels are energy sources that formed when plants and animals died millions of years ago. As their bodies decayed and returned to the earth, they were buried under layers of new soil. The pressure of all those layers pushing down on them formed them into the fossil fuels we use today. There's no way we could replace those in time to use them again, unless we can hang around another several million years. Once we've used up these fossil fuels we'll have to use other energy sources to power our world.

That's why it's so important for us to conserve our sources of energy, as well as develop new sources. Once we burn through the existing **fossil fuels** by using gasoline in our vehicles or burning coal to generate electricity, we'll face a problem—no energy. If everyone pitches in and tries to cut back on how much energy we use now, our supply will last a little longer. Hopefully scientists will come up with some better ways to use renewable energy sources before our fossil fuels run out! Right now renewables are often too expensive to use instead of fossil fuels.

Ideally, everything in our world that needs energy should be powered by a renewable energy source. That way we'd never run out. But unfortunately, too much of our energy comes from non-renewable sources like fossil fuels.

Why do we keep using fossil fuels if we're going to run out? For one thing, they're cheap to gather compared to other energy sources. It only costs hundreds of dollars to buy enough electricity generated from fossil fuels to power a whole house for a year. To purchase and install enough solar panels to power your whole house using energy from the sun would cost tens of thousands of dollars.

Words to Know

renewable: an energy source that can replenish itself.

non-renewable: energy sources that can be used up, that we can't make more of.

fossil fuels: non-renewable energy sources such as oil, natural gas, and coal. Made from plants and animals that died millions of years ago.

Even though it's hard to break free from fossil fuel use, you can help reduce your own family's consumption. You can:

✔ Ride your bike or walk instead of taking the car.
✔ Turn off lights and appliances when you aren't using them.
✔ Put on a sweater if you're cold or go for a swim if you're hot, rather than cranking the air conditioning or blasting the heater.

A lot of the time, when you save energy, you're also helping the environment. When you save energy resources, you also cut down on the waste products that are created by using them. Some of those waste products are called greenhouse gases.

Greenhouse gases are blamed for global warming. Some scientists believe the earth's temperature is climbing a little bit every year because of greenhouse gases, and they call this temperature rise global warming. Global warming spells trouble for life on Earth. Snow and ice is melting at the North and South Poles and on mountaintops. Some plants and animals are in danger because of rising temperatures. If too much ice melts it will raise water levels in the oceans.

CARRY ME!

You may think electricity is energy. This isn't completely accurate. Electricity is actually an energy carrier. That means that it's not the source of the power itself. It's more like a conveyor belt, shuttling energy from one spot to another.

The next chapter talks about electricity and how it fits into the overall energy picture. Then we'll learn about hydrogen, another energy carrier. After that, the rest of the chapters talk about sources of energy—things that contain energy that we can harness and use to move things or generate electricity or power our vehicles.

NEWTON'S CRADLE

This project will show you how energy is transferred between objects. When the first bead hits the second bead, it transfers its kinetic energy. The second bead transfers the kinetic energy to the third bead, which starts moving.

1. Cut three pieces of string, each about a foot long. Thread each piece of string through one bead, then loop the string around the bead a few times, going back through the hole each time. Try to keep the bead as close to the center of the string as possible, but it doesn't have to be exact.

2. Put a large dab of glue or a blob of the clay in the center of the box. Position one bead so it's directly over the clay, then push the bead into the clay or glue, sticking it there firmly.

3. Tape the ends of the string onto both sides of the box, making the string taut. Be sure the bead stays stuck.

4. Lower one of the other beads into the box so it's on one side of the stuck bead, just barely touching it, but not touching the bottom of the box. Tape the bead's string tightly in place.

5. Lower the third bead so it's on the other side of the stuck bead, also gently touching the stuck bead but not touching the bottom of the box. Tape this bead's string tightly in place.

supplies

- scissors
- string or thread
- 3 beads with holes in the center, all the same size
- glue or clay
- shoebox
- tape

6. All three beads should be touching each other, with the middle bead the only one resting on the bottom of the box.

7. Gently pull back one of the outside beads and release it. The first bead will hit the middle bead, passing its kinetic energy through this bead to the remaining one—which will fly away!

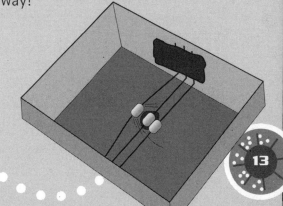

Make Your Own

SIMPLE ENERGY

With this simple car, you'll see the difference between stored energy and kinetic energy. When the rubber band is twisted tight, it's packed with potential energy—stored up and ready for anything. When you release the rubber band, the potential energy is converted into kinetic energy—and your car moves. Try different sizes of rubber bands to see the difference in output.

supplies

- 2 straws
- duct tape
- small box or container like a milk carton
- scissors
- 2 skewers or dowels a little longer than the width of the box
- CDs or yogurt container tops with holes in the middle
- clay
- rubber bands
- thumbtack
- stickers, markers, glitter, and other items to decorate your car

1. Tape one straw to the bottom of the container about an inch from one of the short edges. This will be the front of your car.

2. Cut the other straw into two short pieces. Line up the two pieces of straw on the bottom of the container toward the back, also about an inch from the edge. They should be in line with each other, but with about an inch of space between them. You may have to trim the ends if they stick too far past the edge. Tape them down very tightly.

3. Push one skewer through the straws in the back and another through the straw in the front. These are your axles.

4. Secure the CDs on each end of the skewers. The CD holes will be larger than your skewer, so you'll have to fill in the space with clay.

CAR

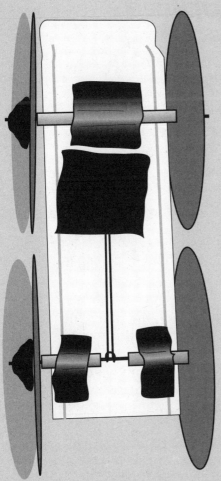

5. Loop the rubber band around the rear skewer in the space between the straws. An easy way to do this is to push the rubber band under the skewer, then run it back through the loop on the other side of the dowel and pull tight.

6. Pull the rubber band toward the front of the container. Don't stretch it so far that it won't stretch any more, because you won't be able to twist it when you're ready to roll.

7. Secure the rubber band to the bottom of the box using the thumbtack. Tape over the tack with duct tape to make sure it's extra secure. Decorate your car, and it's ready to roll!

8. To make your car go, turn the back wheels until the rubber band is twisted around the rear axle and ready to spring. Set your car down, and let it go. Experiment by setting the car at the bottom of a ramp to see how much energy it needs to go up inclines. See if it has enough energy to launch off jumps.

ENERGY CONVERTER

How is heat really a form of energy? A bottle and a coin can show you. This project also makes a really cool magic trick!

supplies

- empty glass bottle with cap removed
- refrigerator
- small bowl full of water
- quarter

1. Put the bottle in the refrigerator for about 15 minutes.

2. Remove the bottle and dip the top into the water to get it wet.

3. Dip the coin in the water, then set it on the top of the bottle's mouth.

4. Grip the bottle tightly between your hands. Be careful not to jostle the bottle around. You don't want the coin to slip off.

5. As your body heat warms up the air inside the bottle, the air will expand—and make the coin on the top of the bottle wiggle!

Chapter 2
Electricity

When you walk into a dark room, you can flip a switch and instantly have light. You can push a button and turn on a computer, reach into your cold refrigerator for a gallon of milk, or listen to music on a radio. You can do these things thanks to electricity. But what is electricity, really?

Electricity isn't a *source* of energy—it's a *carrier* of energy. Mechanical or chemical energy is converted into electrical energy, something that we can harness and use in our everyday lives.

Although humans can create electricity, it's also present in nature—just think about a storm with lightning. Lightning is an electrical charge. How about when you shuffle across a carpet, reach out a finger, and zzzap!—shock your brother. These are forms of electricity too, called **static electricity**.

... BUT WHAT IS IT?

To understand electricity, you have to zoom in to see matter close up—way, way in, to look at molecules. Remember, molecules are the microscopic pieces that make up matter. And molecules are made of even smaller pieces—atoms. If you zoomed in close enough to see the atoms, you'd realize that even atoms are made of smaller parts.

a molecule

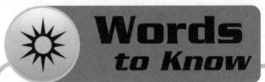

A positive electrical charge attracts a negative electrical charge.

atom

atom   atom

atom   atom

atom   atom

Every atom has a center, called a **nucleus**. And the nucleus is made up of even smaller bits called **neutrons** and **protons**. Circling around the nucleus, like tiny flies, are particles called **electrons**.

But all these little bits aren't identical. The protons and electrons each carry their own power, their own electrical charge. The protons have a positive charge, and the electrons have a negative charge. The neutrons have no charge, so they are "neutral."

If you're familiar with magnets, you know that they have a positive end and a negative end. These are sometimes marked with a little plus sign for positive charge and a minus sign for negative charge. If you bring the positive ends of two magnets close together, they'll **repel** each other. That's because one positive charge pushes away another positive charge. Negative charges work the same way. But the negative charge on one magnet will be attracted to the positive charge on the other. The ends will be pulled toward each other with a force.

Words to Know

static electricity: a build-up of an electric charge on an object.

nucleus: the center of an atom.

neutrons: the particles in the nucleus with no charge.

protons: the particles in the nucleus with a positive electrical charge.

electrons: the particles in the atom with a negative electrical charge that circle around the nucleus.

repel: to resist or push away.

orbit: a repeating path that circles around something else.

Atoms work in the same manner. The electrons with their negative charge are attracted to the protons with their positive charge. The protons are pulled toward the electrons. Opposites attract.

inside an atom

neutrons

electrons

protons

Unlike magnets, electrons and protons don't actually touch each other. That's because around each nucleus (where the protons are), there are **orbits** of space. And that's where the electrons stay—inside their orbits, unable to come closer to the nucleus. Each orbit holds electrons. An atom is like an onion, with many circular layers. You have the very center of the atom, where the nucleus is. Then you have the first orbit, with two electrons. Then another orbit, with more electrons, and so on. The simplest atom, hydrogen, has just one electron. But other atoms have many more electrons. An atom can have up to eight orbits.

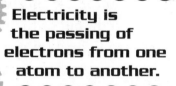

Electricity is the passing of electrons from one atom to another.

So what does all this have to do with electricity? Plenty. Think about the two magnets again. If you're holding the two magnets close to each other, you can feel the strong force between them, pulling them together. But what if you move them farther away? It's harder to feel the force between them.

Did you know?

If you had a light switch in your bedroom that could turn on a light on the moon, it would take just over one second for it to light up—that's how fast electricity travels. You'd need a lot of wire, though!

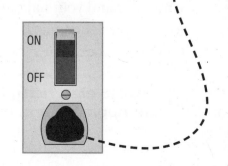

ON

OFF

WATT'S IT ALL ABOUT?

There are several different ways to measure electricity:

* **Volts** are kind of like water pressure, only it's electrical "pressure" you're measuring! The more volts something has, the more "intense" or forceful it is.

* **Watts** measure how much energy is being consumed by an electrical object. For example, a traditional light bulb uses energy at a rate of 25 to 100 watts, and a fluorescent light bulb burns energy at a rate of 5 to 30 watts. The traditional light bulb uses more energy.

* **Ohms** measure the amount of resistance to the electrical current. Think of resistance like a small water pipe. Only so much water can flow through it. But if you increase the size of the pipe, more water can easily flow at one time. You've taken away the resistance. Ohms measure how hard it is for the electricity to flow.

* **Amps** measure the electrical current, or the amount of electrons flowing per second.

The same thing happens with electrons. Electrons in the orbits farther from the nucleus have a weaker force pulling them toward the protons. If another force is applied to them they can "jump ship" and get knocked right out of their orbits, onto another atom, because the force pulling them is so light. That passing of electrons from one atom to another is electricity. And there are two kinds of electricity: static electricity and current electricity.

STATIC ELECTRICITY

Remember that zap you gave your brother after shuffling across the carpet? That's static electricity, and that was a bunch of electrons jumping off of you and onto your brother. You can experience static electricity in a lot of different ways. If you've ever taken off your hat on a winter day and your hair stood on end, that's static electricity. Or if you've gone down a slide, and afterwards you reached out to touch someone and received a shock, that's static electricity, too.

Static electricity is formed when the balance between the negative and positive charges in an object is uneven.

The charges build up on the surface of that object until they find another place to jump to or a way to be released. When you're shuffling your feet, you're picking up electrons off the carpet. They're gathering up in your body and pushing against each other. Remember, charges that are alike push away from each other. When you take your hat off, the charges on your hair want to push away from each other, so the hairs stand on end to get as far as possible away from each other!

Another form of static electricity is lightning. Scientists believe that ice crystals inside clouds rub up against each other, building a negative charge in the cloud. On the ground, a positive charge builds up. Finally, the charges are so strong that they attract—and electrons jump between the cloud and the ground, or between different clouds.

When the charges move, the air is so hot that it glows. This is the lightning bolt you see. The hot air expands so fast it creates an explosive noise that you hear as thunder.

Did you know?

In less than one second, a bolt of lightning generates up to 3 million volts of electricity!

CURRENT ELECTRICITY

Current electricity is a steady flow of electrons along a path. It always needs to have a complete path to move the electrons along. If the path is broken, the electrons won't move, and electricity won't flow. The complete path is called a **circuit.** This word comes from the word for circle, so you can picture a complete path without interruption.

An example of a simple circuit is a light bulb. When you turn the light on, you're completing the circuit—the electrons flow and the light glows. And when you turn the light off, you're breaking, or disconnecting, the circuit, so the electrons don't move. And you don't get any light.

A "direct current," or DC for short, is one in which the electrons flow in one direction. An "alternating current," or AC, is a circuit where the electrons flow both ways.

WHAT'S THE CURRENT SITUATION?

When electrons are flowing, you have a current of electricity. If they're all moving in the same direction, like a one-way street, you have "direct current," or DC. But if they all move in one direction, and then change direction together and flow the other way, you've got "alternating current," or AC. You use AC the most at home—it's what comes in through the outlet when you plug something in. DC is the electricity that comes from batteries. But why are there two types?

Thomas Edison invented DC power when he realized that a magnet near a wire made the electrons move in a single direction. But the problem with DC is that it weakens over distances. So your home would have to be pretty close to the energy station to use the electricity.

Nikola Tesla invented AC power when he rotated the magnet, making the electrons flow first in one direction, then the other. AC replaced DC in powering homes because AC can travel over long distances easily.

BATTERY CHARGE

So where do batteries fit into this? You know that sometimes stuff that runs on electricity—things you plug in—can also be run from batteries instead. That's because batteries are little storage containers. What do they store? Current electricity! When you use batteries, you're tapping into their supplies of stored electricity. Batteries work for things that are never plugged in, too, because some things are made to work just from batteries. When your flashlight runs out of power, you pop in a fresh set of batteries, and voilà! You have light.

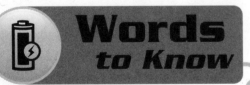

Words to Know

circuit: a complete path of an electrical current.

terminals: positive and negative contact points on a battery.

turbine: a machine that turns when a force is applied to it, sending mechanical energy to a generator.

generator: a machine that converts mechanical energy into electricity.

The circuit in a battery has to be complete for it to work.

But how do those little canisters pack such an electric punch? A chemical solution and metal in the battery creates electricity.

Here's how batteries work:

* Batteries have two contact points, or **terminals**. One is marked with a plus sign (+), which means that's the positive terminal. The other is marked with a minus sign (-), which means it's the negative terminal.

* Chemicals that are inside the battery mix together, producing electrons.

* Those electrons gather on the negative terminal of the battery, ready to flow (or form an electric current) if a wire touches it and gives it a pathway.

* The positive terminal of the battery is where the electrons return after their journey through an electrical circuit. Remember, a circuit has to be complete in order for it to work. If you just had a wire connected to the negative terminal of the battery, nothing would happen because it's not a complete circuit, just a dead end.

Did you know?

Some fish can actually generate electricity themselves. Electric eels can generate nearly 650 volts!

ENERGY

LET THERE BE POWER!

You've learned that energy is the ability to do work. You've also learned that there are several different sources of energy. How do we convert these sources into electricity?

✳ Energy that comes from any source—solar, wind, nuclear, fossil fuels—can be converted into electricity through a **turbine** and a **generator**. There are several steps involved. A turbine is a machine that works because a force is applied to it, making it move. It usually has a shaft connected to paddles on one end. Those paddles are moved by the energy source. For example, if the energy source is water rushing over a dam, the water turns the paddles, and the paddles turn the shaft, making it spin. When wind turns a windmill, the windmill turns the turbine. The spinning of the turbine creates mechanical energy.

✳ Once the turbine is spinning, that mechanical energy is transformed into electricity by the generator. A generator is basically a wire and a giant magnet. When the wire is turned, the magnet forces the electrons inside the wire to start moving—which is the current of electricity.

✳ When fossil fuels are burned it creates heat. Heat energy is the rapid movement of molecules. We use heat energy in many ways, but to generate electricity, the heat energy boils water, producing steam that turns the turbine. Fossil fuels have been converted to heat energy, which is then converted to mechanical energy.

A turbine is a series of blades. It is often made of steel, but sometimes ceramic. This is a material that can withstand higher temperatures.

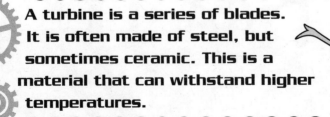

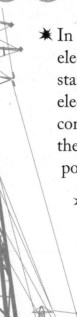

✴ In the same way, chemical energy can be converted to electricity. In batteries, chemicals are mixed together, starting a flow of electrons. That electron flow is the electricity that powers your flashlight or makes a remote control car speed across the ground. Electric cars work the same way, using a very large battery to produce more power.

✴ A generator takes the energy that's been captured through mechanical, solar, or heat energy and converts it into the electricity that we use for all kinds things, from lights and cell phones, to computers and microwave ovens. You'll learn more details about how each of the energy sources work in later chapters.

GENERATE SOME ACTION!

No matter how the electricity is formed, it follows the same path to your house. At the power plant, electricity is created. Then the electricity is sent through wires to a switchyard where the voltage is increased so the electricity can travel long distances.

The electricity is distributed to many transmission lines, which are the really big power lines you see with many wires coming into them. Electricity travels along these wires until it's close to your home or other destination. Then it's sent through a substation where the voltage is reduced back down. After the substation, the electricity moves along through smaller distribution lines. These are the wires strung between wooden poles you see everywhere along the road. But there's one more stop before the electricity reaches your house. It has to go through a transformer to be reduced a bit more in voltage.

If it wasn't for the transformer reducing the voltage, the electricity would blow out all of your appliances! Finally, the electricity travels through wires into your home. You finish the journey when you plug in an electronic device to the outlet in your wall.

JUMPING FROGS

Use the power of static electricity to animate a bunch of little frogs! You'll create an imbalance of electrons, then watch as those electrons make your frogs jump!

supplies

- construction paper
- scissors
- markers
- balloon

1. Cut several little frogs out of the construction paper. Don't make them too big—no more than about 2 inches each. Decorate your frogs with fun designs. Then scatter them on a table or countertop.

2. Blow up the balloon. Rub the balloon against a sweater, blanket, or even your hair.

3. Hold the balloon over the frogs. The static charge between the balloon and the paper frogs will attract the frogs, and they'll start jumping up to try to grab on to the balloon.

SIMPLE LEMON BATTERY

The acid in lemons and citrus fruits reacts with metals (in this case, coins) to create chemical energy. Protons are pulled to one metal, and electrons are pulled to the other. Ask an adult to help you with the knife.

supplies

- lemon
- knife
- one penny
- one dime
- thin copper wire
- compass
- miniature light bulb

1. Squeeze your lemon and roll it around between your palm and a table. This will loosen up the juices and get everything flowing well inside the fruit.

2. Cut two small slits in the top of the lemon, just long enough to hold your coins. Ask an adult for help if you're using a sharp knife. Insert the penny into one slot and the dime into the other.

3. Wrap the copper wire around the compass, leaving plenty of wire on each end. Wrap one end of the wire around the penny, and the other end around the dime.

4. As you make the final connection around the second coin, watch the compass needle. When you make the connection, it will jump. This shows you that electricity is flowing through the wire. You've completed the circuit.

5. Now use two wires. Attach one to the penny and the light bulb. Attach the other wire to the light bulb and the dime. The light should glow from your electric lemon!

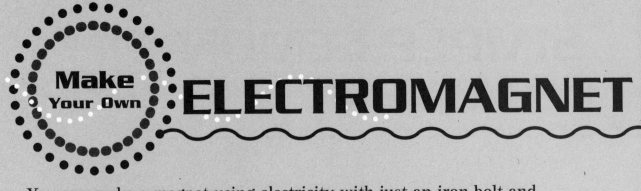

You can make a magnet using electricity with just an iron bolt and a battery. When an electric current moves through the wire around the bolt, it creates a magnetic field in the bolt.

supplies

- iron bolt
- copper wire
- D battery
- electrical tape
- small metal objects such as nails or paper clips

1. Wrap the wire around the bolt. The more times you wind it around the bolt, the stronger the force will be. Try to wrap it at least 20 times and even more if you can. Leave a few inches of extra wire hanging at each end.

2. Use the tape to connect the wire to the battery. Connect one end of the wire to the positive terminal of the battery, and the other end of the wire to the negative terminal of the battery.

3. See if you can pick up things with your iron bolt—it's an electromagnet and will attract metal objects. Try disconnecting the battery while you're attracting objects and see what happens to the magnetic force. When you disconnect the battery you break the circuit. This stops the flow of electrons.

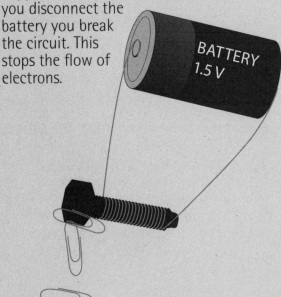

BATTERY 1.5 V

Chapter 3
Hydrogen

What has no color, no smell, is lighter than air, and makes up almost 75 percent of the universe? It's the **element** hydrogen. An element is a kind of matter that is made of all the same atoms. There are lots of other elements that you've heard of, such as oxygen and sodium. Oxygen is in the air we breathe and sodium is in salt.

Hydrogen is the most basic element we know of. A single atom of hydrogen has one proton, one electron, and no neutrons. Other elements have more electrons and protons. Oxygen has eight electrons. Sodium has 11.

hydrogen atom

−
Electron

+
Proton

Hydrogen is in almost everything. For example, you probably know that another name for water is H_2O. This is water's chemical formula. It represents one water **molecule**. H is the symbol for hydrogen and O is the symbol for oxygen. That means that every molecule of water is made up of two hydrogen atoms and one oxygen atom.

Words to Know

element: a very basic substance from which other things are made. A substance with all the same atoms. The number of protons in an atom determines what kind of atom it is.

molecule: a group of atoms bound together. Molecules combine to form matter.

atmosphere: the gases that surround the earth.

electrolysis: the process used to capture hydrogen from water using electricity.

methane: a gas with no color or smell made from natural sources.

Hydrogen can combine with just about every other element scientists know about. When it combines with carbon, it can form fossil fuels. And it's present in every living thing, even you!

But hydrogen doesn't exist on Earth by itself. That's because hydrogen by itself is hydrogen gas, and hydrogen gas is lighter than air. It just drifts away up into the **atmosphere**. To get hydrogen it has to be "pulled out" or "captured" from substances that contain it, like water or methane gas.

Stars are made mostly of hydrogen. The hydrogen atoms in our star, the sun, combine to form helium atoms—another element. This produces light, called radiant energy.

GOTCHA! CAPTURING HYDROGEN

Like electricity, hydrogen can be used as an energy carrier. We can use sources of energy like fossil fuels and water to make hydrogen. Hydrogen is easy to use, but first you have to capture it. One way is to pull hydrogen out of water. With a process called **electrolysis**, the atoms in water—hydrogen and oxygen—can be separated. The hydrogen atoms can then be collected. This is expensive, though.

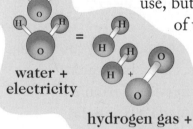

water + electricity = hydrogen gas + oxygen

Another way to capture hydrogen is to split the hydrogen from a carbon-based material, like **methane** gas. When steam and methane are combined, the products are carbon monoxide and hydrogen. A big problem with this method is that carbon monoxide pollutes the atmosphere.

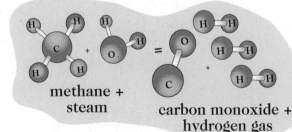

methane + steam = carbon monoxide + hydrogen gas

Did you know?

In 2007, a man in Florida named John Kanzius found he could separate hydrogen from salt water using radio waves. Then he could burn it as a fuel.

HOW IT'S USED

Once hydrogen has been captured, it's ready to go to work transporting energy. This is done using **fuel cells**. Fuel cells generate electricity through a chemical reaction between hydrogen and oxygen, using oxygen that's pulled from the air. The fuel cells operate like batteries in that they convert chemical energy to electrical energy. The electricity generated by the fuel cells can then be stored in a battery, ready to use.

HOW FUEL CELLS WORK

Words to Know

fuel cell: something that produces a steady stream of electricity.

Proton Exchange Membrane (PEM): a compact fuel cell that can power cars. One fuel cell doesn't provide enough energy to run a car, so several PEMs are piled together into one unit called a stack.

There are different kinds of fuel cells. One that can be used for running cars is called a **Proton Exchange Membrane (PEM)** fuel cell. PEM fuel cells are shaped like sandwiches and have four parts.

- **Anode.** This is like the negative post on a battery. Electrons are freed from the hydrogen and conducted out to the electrical circuit.
- **Cathode.** This is like the positive post on a battery, and it conducts the electrons back from the circuit to the catalyst.
- **Catalyst.** The catalyst is a special material that helps the oxygen and hydrogen interact.
- **Electrolyte:** The electrolyte is the PEM, the barrier that allows the protons to pass through but not the electrons.

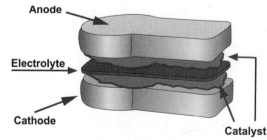

Anode

Electrolyte

Cathode

Catalyst

NASA uses hydrogen fuel cells to generate electricity on the space shuttle. The waste product is water, which the astronauts use as drinking water.

The anode and cathode are like the pieces of bread, with the PEM—the **membrane**—in the middle like the filling. Here's how it all works:

- First, hydrogen is channeled to the anode from the tank where it's stored.

- A catalyst at the anode splits the hydrogen into electrons and protons, the positive and negative parts of the hydrogen atom. The positively charged protons pass through the PEM. The electrons can't pass through the PEM because it lets only protons through.

- The electrons move off, forming the movement of electrons that becomes the electrical current. They're now providing electricity to the circuit.

- In the meantime, the protons arrive at the cathode, on the other side of the "sandwich."

- While all this is going on, oxygen has been arriving at the cathode side. The oxygen meets up with the protons and the electrons that are returning from their journey around the circuit. The oxygen, the hydrogen protons, and the electrons combine, and form water.

- The water flows out of the cell as a "waste" product, either in liquid form or as water vapor. It leaves the fuel cell like greenhouse gases leave a traditional **combustion engine** burning gasoline.

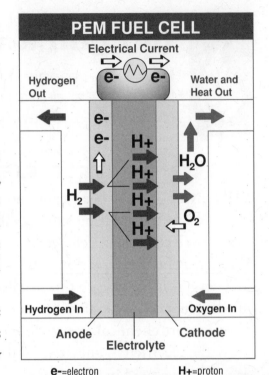

PEM FUEL CELL

Electrical Current

e-   e-

Hydrogen Out   Water and Heat Out

e-
e-   e-   H+
                H+   H₂O
H₂   H+
                H+   O₂
                H+

Hydrogen In   Oxygen In

Anode   Electrolyte   Cathode

e-=electron   H+=proton

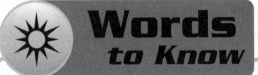

Words to Know

anode: where electrons are separated from hydrogen in a fuel cell.

cathode: where the electrons return from the circuit in a fuel cell.

catalyst: something that causes a chemical reaction.

electrolyte: the membrane that controls the flow of protons.

membrane: thin material that allows some materials to pass through but not others. In a fuel cell it allows protons to pass through.

combustion engine: a heat engine that burns fuel.

THE ADVANTAGES AND DISADVANTAGES OF HYDROGEN AS AN ENERGY CARRIER

Some people see hydrogen as the energy carrier of the future. Some of the benefits of hydrogen are:

- A hydrogen-powered vehicle is much quieter than one with a traditional engine.
- The output, or waste product, is water. This is a very clean "waste," and one that can be taken back into the **water cycle** and reused.
- A hydrogen-powered vehicle works more efficiently than a traditional, combustion engine that runs on gasoline. More energy is produced than it uses. A traditional engine needs larger amounts of energy to do the same amount of work.

But hydrogen isn't a miracle energy carrier just yet. There are some drawbacks:

- It's expensive to produce hydrogen. Since hydrogen is an energy carrier, first we have to make it. That's why we don't use it yet.

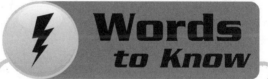

water cycle: the endless process that water travels through on Earth. It evaporates to become water vapor in clouds. Then it condenses into liquid water in the form of rain or snow, over and over again.

- It's really hard to store hydrogen, unlike traditional gasoline, which is easily stored.
- It will take time and money to make hydrogen fuel readily available for people to use. Right now, virtually everyone uses fossil fuels for their energy needs. Converting everything, like car engines and electrical plants, will take lots of effort.

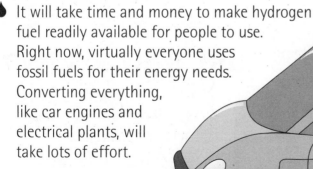

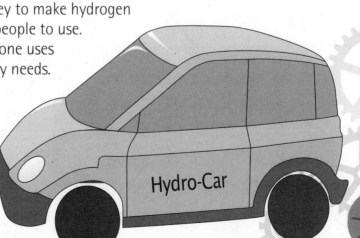

Hydro-Car

Make Your Own HYDROGEN

It's possible to make hydrogen yourself! What you're actually doing is pulling hydrogen out of water. This is called electrolysis. Since water is made up of two hydrogen atoms connected to a single oxygen atom (H_2O), you're breaking apart the water by using a small current of electricity. The hydrogen breaks free from the oxygen molecules and floats to the top because it's very light.

supplies

- table salt
- glass of water
- 2 pieces of bare copper wire, each about 5 inches long
- 9-volt battery

1. Stir about 2 teaspoons of table salt into the water until it's all dissolved.

2. Wrap one end of each wire around a terminal on the 9-volt battery. Don't touch the ends of the wires together.

3. Place the other ends of the wire into the water. Don't let these ends of the wire touch each other either.

4. Watch what happens. The bubbles that appear and float to the surface are molecules of hydrogen gas.

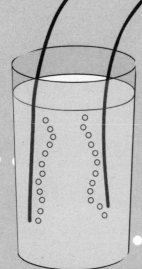

Did you know?

Hydrogen was named in 1783 after Greek words that basically mean "water generating."

Chapter 4
Petroleum

Whether you call it black gold, **petroleum**, or oil, this thick, sticky, black fluid is one of the most valuable resources on the planet. That's because so much of our everyday lives rely on it. Oil fuels cars, airplanes, buses, and other modes of transportation. It heats our homes and businesses. And it is used to make all kinds of products that we need, such as paints and plastics. Look around. What would your life be like without plastic?

Oil was used in early times in America, too. Native Americans were known to use oil to waterproof their canoes. And oil was used to light lamps when the price of whale oil grew too high in the 1800s. The Chinese even used petroleum in lamps 2,000 year ago!

Petroleum is a non-renewable energy source.

35

A LONG, LONG TIME AGO...

Oil is a fossil fuel. That means it's made from fossils, which are the remains of creatures that lived millions of years ago. Way back before people walked the earth, tiny plants and animals floated around in the seas that covered our planet.

Did you know?

Oil is measured in barrels. A barrel contains 42 gallons. The United States uses the most oil in the world—about 20 million barrels each day. That's 840 million gallons of oil every single day!

When they died, the plants and animals settled on the bottom of the sea. As the years passed, more and more creatures piled up and were buried in layer upon layer of sand, mud, and clay.

In time, the oceans receded. That mud and sand turned into rock, and that rock pressed down on the creatures' remains. The heat that exists deep under the ground and the pressure of layers and layers of rocks pushing down from above combined to form a "pressure cooker." Over millions of years this pressure-cooker compressed and decayed the remains until they became tiny drops of liquid. That liquid is the oil we use today.

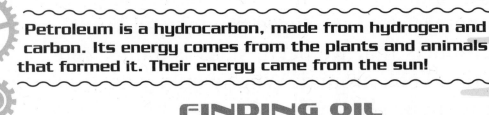

Petroleum is a hydrocarbon, made from hydrogen and carbon. Its energy comes from the plants and animals that formed it. Their energy came from the sun!

FINDING OIL

Sometimes oil oozes out of the ground. But most oil is deep underground, in pockets in the rock buried beneath the earth's surface.

Where there's oil, there is usually another fossil fuel called natural gas. The gas is lighter and floats to the surface of the oil. Certain places around the globe have these oil and gas deposits. Some of the oil and gas layers are located under the ocean, while others are found under the land. A few countries have "struck it rich" and have very large supplies.

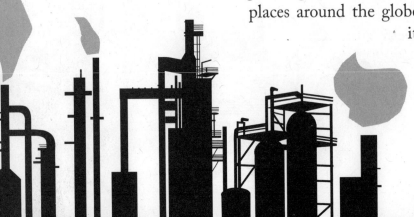

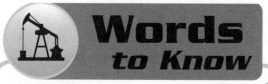

Words to Know

petroleum: another word for oil.

permeable: a substance that liquid (or gas) can flow through.

seismograph: an instrument that measures vibrations under the ground.

Scientists have found oil everywhere on the planet—except in frozen Antarctica. More than half of the oil in the whole world is in the Middle East. The Middle East is the region between Africa and India. The countries that produce the most oil are Russia, Saudi Arabia, the United States, China, Iran, Iraq, Mexico, and Canada. Saudi Arabia, Iran, and Iraq are all in the Middle East. In the United States, Texas produces the most oil, followed by Alaska and California.

Locating oil is a job for geologists, who are scientists that study rocks. They can take special photos from up in airplanes and satellites, trying to locate the areas of land that look most likely to have layers of **permeable** rock. This is rock that liquids like

Did you know?

The word petroleum comes from the latin words "petra" and "oleum" that mean rock and oil. The word "petroleum" can also refer to gas.

oil can flow through. Another way they can locate oil is by measuring shock waves through the ground using a **seismograph**. Scientists set off small "shock waves" or bursts of energy that travel down through the rock layers. When the waves bounce back up to the surface, the scientists try to interpret what those waves are telling them. They're trying to locate "pockets" in the rock—spaces that aren't solid.

These pockets could be filled with oil. A shock wave that hits a pocket might bounce back weaker than the initial wave. A wave that hits nothing but solid rock would bounce back stronger. Think of throwing a rubber ball against a surface. If you throw it against a brick wall, it will return to you forcefully. But if you throw the ball into a couch cushion, it will bounce back much less forcefully.

ENERGY

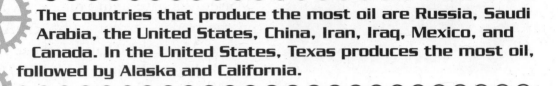

The countries that produce the most oil are Russia, Saudi Arabia, the United States, China, Iran, Iraq, Mexico, and Canada. In the United States, Texas produces the most oil, followed by Alaska and California.

STRIKING OIL

Maybe you've seen a movie or television show where people are drilling for oil and suddenly it comes bursting out of the ground, gushing straight into the air like a geyser. That's actually how it can happen. Oil is under so much pressure, sitting underneath all those layers of rocks, that when a drill punctures a hole through the rocks and gives the oil a place to go, it comes shooting out as fast as it can.

To get the oil out of the ground, companies set up an **oil rig** directly over the place they want to drill for the oil. If that place is under the ocean then that's where the oil rig has to be. Out at sea, the oil rig has to be on a giant platform, large enough to house the workers and the machinery that's needed to drill for oil.

Oil rigs on land look a little like a hammer nailing the ground. The oil rig grinds away at the rock covering the oil deposit with a drill. The **drill bit** at the tip is incredibly strong, since it has to chew through very hard layers of rock. There's no single pipe that's long enough to drill all the way down to many of the deposits, so as the drill bit gets deeper and deeper into the ground, workers connect additional lengths of pipe to the drill to keep it moving.

Once they've hit oil pockets, the workers use pumps to bring the oil to the surface. The oil that comes out of the ground is called **crude oil**. This crude oil is transported from the oil field by huge tankers or by pipeline.

Words to Know

oil rig: a large drill that punctures the earth where oil is, making a hole that allows oil to be brought to the surface.

drill bit: the very hard tip of the drill that grinds through layers of rock.

crude oil: oil in its natural form, right out of the ground.

refinery: factory where petroleum is separated into different oil types.

BUT FIRST...

Before the oil can be used, it has to be processed. The tankers and pipelines deliver crude oil to **refineries**. A refinery is a factory where crude oil is processed into parts, or components, that will be used in different ways. Liquids and vapors inside the refinery separate the oil into its unique components. Because each of those components has a different weight or thickness, they separate naturally.

It's kind of like mixing sugar in water. If you wait, the sugar will eventually settle on the bottom because it's heavier than water. Gasoline and liquid petroleum gas floats to the top because it's the lightest. Then comes jet and diesel fuel. Gas oils are heavier still, so they're at the bottom.

Oil goes into making all kinds of things like crayons, deodorant, shower doors, toilet seats, candles, footballs, balloons, tires, toothpaste, and fishing lures.

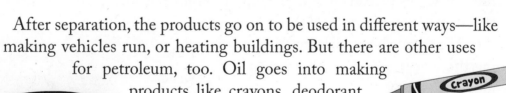

After separation, the products go on to be used in different ways—like making vehicles run, or heating buildings. But there are other uses for petroleum, too. Oil goes into making products like crayons, deodorant, shower doors, toilet seats, candles, footballs, balloons, tires, toothpaste, and fishing lures.

MAKING CARS GO

Gasoline is the most common form of fuel for cars. It's very important to our current lifestyle and our economy. (And to think, it was formed from a bunch of tiny creatures millions of years ago!)

GREENHOUSE GASES AND GLOBAL WARMING

In a healthy environment, the earth's atmosphere traps some of the sun's energy close to the planet while letting the rest of it radiate back into the universe. That's what keeps Earth at a comfortable living temperature. It's like a cozy blanket. But when fossil fuels are burned, they release gases like carbon dioxide into the air. These gases are called greenhouse gases. They kind of clog the atmosphere, making our "cozy blanket" more like a fat, heavy quilt that's way too warm. The gases build up over time with no place to go. They make the overall temperature of the planet rise a tiny bit each year. This is called global warming.

A combination of fuel, fire, and air makes your car go. The car's engine is called a combustion engine, because the gasoline in the engine is burned to create power. The gasoline is combined with oxygen and a spark (the "fire") is provided by spark plugs. The result is lots of heat, water, and carbon dioxide. It's like a mini explosion, and that explosion forces **pistons** in a car's engine to move up and down. As they move up and down, the mechanical parts of the car's engine begin moving, turning the wheels and making your car move.

The carbon dioxide that is sent out as waste through the exhaust pipe is what contributes to the greenhouse gases that bother our planet. Greenhouse gases contribute to global warming. It's one of the disadvantages of burning fossil fuels.

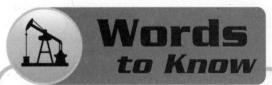

Words to Know

pistons: sliding pieces that move up and down or back and forth.

environment: an area that includes plants and animals.

sorbent: a material that can absorb a liquid or semi-liquid.

A STICKY PROBLEM

Sometimes, when crude oil is being transported, accidents happen. Giant ocean tankers that are transporting petroleum can leak or spill the oil. And when that happens, the **environment** is at risk. Oil is lighter than water, so it floats on the surface in a thick, choking blanket of blackness. Marine animals like seals or otters become coated in the gooey mess and can't clean themselves off. They swallow the oil and die. Birds can't clean off the oil that coats their feathers, so they can't fly and find food for themselves.

Cleaning up oil spills is a major headache. It's tough to contain it when it's floating on the ocean's tides, and when it washes ashore, it sticks like a layer of black glue to rocks, beaches, and plants. Different **sorbents** can clean up some of the spill. But the problems can last for years and affect an area for a long time, because all the oil can't possibly be removed.

THE ADVANTAGES AND DISADVANTAGES OF OIL

There are some advantages to using oil as an energy source:

- It's relatively cheap because the systems for retrieving and distributing the oil have been established for so long.

- It's portable and can be stored easily.

Some of the disadvantages are:

- It's a non-renewable fossil fuel. Since there's a limited supply of petroleum, eventually we'll run out. It takes millions of years for plants and animals to decay and form into oil. Some scientists estimate that we may run out in less than 30 years!

- Countries go to war over oil. That's one of the reasons there is so much fighting in the Middle East.

- Burning oil contributes to global warming.

- Oil spills cause severe environmental problems.

Make Your Own

OIL SPILL EXPERIMENT

If you're having a hard time imagining just how hard it is to clean up an oil spill, try this project.

supplies

- 9-by-13-inch glass baking dish
- water
- blue food coloring
- stirring stick or a spoon
- cup
- vegetable oil
- cocoa powder
- things to clean the "oil spill" such as cotton balls, a cup, paper towels, peat moss—these are your "sorbents"
- bird feather

1. Fill the baking dish with water. Add some blue food coloring to tint the water so you can see it more clearly. Mix until the coloring is dispersed evenly. Set aside.

2. In the cup, mix together 3 tablespoons of vegetable oil and 2 tablespoons of the cocoa powder. Mix until it's well blended. This is your crude oil.

3. Very slowly pour the crude oil onto your water. Make sure you take your time and "ease" the oil onto the surface of the water so it floats, but doesn't mix in.

4. Use your sorbents to see which work the best—and which don't work at all. As you're trying each, ask yourself how hard it would be to clean an entire area of the ocean with that material.

5. Finally, take your bird feather and dip it in your oil spill or coat it with vegetable oil. The feather will separate into sections and look very ragged. You can see how hard it would be for a bird to fly with its feathers like that. How could it clean itself off?

Did you know?

About 6 million tons of petroleum end up in the earth's waters every year.

Chapter 5
Natural Gas

All those organisms that died millions of years ago and were transformed into petroleum also created something else. Natural gas. You remember that petroleum was formed when those tiny plants and animals died? When they settled into the mud and sand at the bottom of the oceans and in time were pressed under many layers of rock?

methane molecule

Well, as that petroleum was developing, there were also little bubbles of gas that rose through it. These little bubbles are natural gas, mostly made out of **methane**. Methane is a hydrocarbon made out of one carbon atom and four hydrogen atoms. All that hydrogen makes natural gas lighter than air. It also means natural gas is very **flammable**.

Words to Know

methane: an odorless gas that's the main ingredient in natural gas.

flammable: something that burns very easily.

43

Some of the natural gas and the petroleum below it rose to the surface of the earth over a long period of time. Both are lighter than the rock and water around

Did you know?

24 percent of all the energy used in the United States comes from natural gas.

it. So if natural gas could find a hole to the surface it would go there. When oil or natural gas breaks through the ground, it's called a seep. Scientists believe that thousands of years ago some of these seeps may have been ignited by lightning. Many ancient civilizations worshipped these "eternal fires." They were awe-inspiring, bursting into flame and continuing to burn for extremely long periods of time. Civilizations realized they could use the natural gas for heat and light.

Natural gas is a non-renewable energy source.

GAS FLOW

Natural gas is found and extracted in much the same way as petroleum. First it has to be located. Different methods include using seismographs to send shock waves through the rock, looking for pockets in the rocks. The geology of an area often provides clues to the location of natural gas deposits. Natural gas is found in the same regions as petroleum—including under the ocean.

Once the deposits are located, drills are sent down to tap them. The gas is then pumped through pipelines to storage areas. Although methane is the primary gas in natural gas, there are other gases that can be separated out. **Propane** is a fuel used in gas grills. **Butane** is bottled and used as a fuel for camp cooking.

WHAT'S THAT SMELL?

Natural gas is invisible and has no smell, and it's also highly flammable. So a chemical is mixed into the natural gas before it's sent into storage tanks. The chemical gives it a really strong smell—like rotten eggs! That way if there is a leak anywhere, either in the process of preparing the gas or in your home, someone will smell it and take care of the leak before there's a big problem, like an explosion.

One of the biggest problems with natural gas is that it's tricky to transport and store. Like air, gas has a tendency to find any tiny leak and drift through it. You can't exactly put gas in a box and ship it.

Pipelines are one of the main ways that natural gas travels to its destination. This is a cheap way to transport gas. A giant network of underground pipes run across the country transporting natural gas. Some of these pipes are about two feet wide! It's hard to have pipelines under the oceans, though.

Did you know?

In 1816, natural gas was first used in the United States to light streetlights in Baltimore.

Natural gas can be burned to create electricity. It is energy efficient because it takes less fuel to generate more energy, and contributes less pollution than burning petroleum or coal.

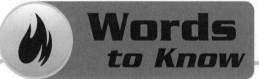

Words to Know

propane: a colorless gas found in natural gas and in crude oil. Often used in cooking.

butane: another flammable gas found in petroleum and natural gas.

compressed: pressed together very tightly, so something takes up less space.

liquefied: when something is changed into a liquid form.

Natural gas can be **compressed**, or **liquefied**. Gases can be liquefied by making them extremely cold. Dropping the temperature of natural gas to about -250 degrees Fahrenheit makes the gas condense into a liquid. That's really cold! It also takes up a lot less space in liquid form. That makes transporting it easier. Liquefied natural gas can cross oceans in big ocean freighters. Tank trucks can transport it. But the two-step process of changing the gas to a liquid, and then the actual transport itself takes more time and costs more.

WHAT'S IT USED FOR?

After the gas is pumped through big pipelines, those pipelines begin to branch off from the larger ones into smaller and smaller sections, like a tree's branches. The smallest ones eventually reach their destinations—homes and businesses. Natural gas has a lot of uses. People can use it to cook food with a gas stove. Half the homes in the United States use natural gas for heat.

Some homes are too far away from the main pipelines for the smaller branches to make any sense. They may use big storage tanks of propane as their heating and cooking source instead.

Although it isn't very common, natural gas can be used as a fuel to power vehicles. When it burns, natural gas provides energy that can move a vehicle. Waste products include carbon dioxide and water vapor. Even though carbon dioxide is a greenhouse gas, natural gas is still considered a "clean-burning" fuel. That's because compared to a gasoline-burning engine, natural gas doesn't emit nearly as many harmful gases.

THE ADVANTAGES AND DISADVANTAGES OF NATURAL GAS

The benefits of using natural gas include:

- ★ It's relatively cheap compared to many renewable energy sources.
- ★ It burns cleaner than petroleum or coal.

Some of the disadvantages include:

- ★ It's non-renewable.
- ★ It's highly flammable, so it can be dangerous to transport and use.
- ★ Natural gas is a little more expensive than the other fossil fuels.
- ★ Burning natural gas produces carbon dioxide and contributes to global warming.

SIMPLE NATURAL GAS

Make Your Own

The only way to make real natural gas is to get the conditions right and wait a couple of million years. But here's a way to mimic the process in a lot less time! What you're actually making with this project is biogas, created when vegetation breaks down. Scientists are working to invent different ways to make this renewable biogas in large quantities. The process is similar to what happened millions of years ago to create natural gas.

supplies

- about 1 cup of soil
- vegetable scraps or grass clippings
- a small plastic bottle such as a water or soda bottle
- small balloon
- duct tape

1. Mix the soil and vegetable scraps or grass clippings together. Put the mixture into your plastic bottle.

2. Stretch the neck of the balloon (don't inflate it) over the bottle, and tape the balloon securely to the bottle.

3. Place the bottle in a place that will get sunlight and be warm. Be sure to keep it protected so it won't tip over or get bumped by people or pets.

4. Check on your bottle, without disturbing it, every day. What's happening to the mixture? What's happening to the balloon?

5. Over time, the mixture will begin to rot. It will give off methane and carbon dioxide gases, which will rise and begin to fill up the balloon. You've made your own natural gas!

Chapter 6
Coal

Coal is a very special rock. That's because it's **combustible**, which means it can catch on fire and burn easily. Naturally, people use it as a source of fuel, heat, and light. Coal is another hydrocarbon, made of carbon, oxygen, and hydrogen. The difference between coal and petroleum is this: while petroleum and natural gas formed from the remains of tiny ancient plants and animals, coal formed from just plants.

Millions of years ago, before and during the time of the dinosaurs, the plants that formed coal grew in swampy areas. When they died, they were buried under layers of soil, silt, sand, and water. Those layers eventually became many layers of heavy rocks that pressed down on the plant remains. In a process similar to the formation of oil and natural gas, the heat of the earth and the pressure of all those layers of heavy rock pressing down on them eventually turned the plants into coal.

When you read the chapter on biomass, you'll learn about a substance called peat. Peat is a material that's made of plants growing in **boggy** conditions. If left alone long enough, peat can turn into coal. They're related, although there's thousands of years of difference in their age!

Not all coal is the same. Coal varies in its hardness, the amount of carbon it contains, and how much heat it can produce. There are four main types of coal:

✳ **Anthracite.** This is the hardest coal with the most carbon. All that carbon gives anthracite the highest energy content of all the types of coal. That means it takes less anthracite to produce energy than it does other kinds of coal. Anthracite is a shiny, black coal found in the northeastern part of Pennsylvania.

✳ **Bituminous.** This dull, black coal has light and dark bands or stripes running through it. Bituminous is mined in the Appalachian Mountain region in the eastern United States.

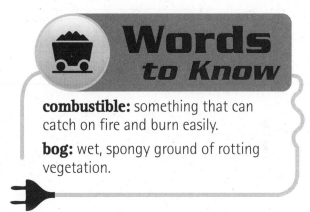

Words to Know

combustible: something that can catch on fire and burn easily.

bog: wet, spongy ground of rotting vegetation.

✳ **Subbituminous.** This coal can range from crumbly to hard. It's not very dense and is mostly used to generate steam-electric power.

✳ **Lignite.** The softest coal, and the lowest in carbon content. It is sometimes called "brown coal" because it's brownish in color. Lignite is crumbly, and very high in hydrogen and oxygen. This type of coal is not as old as the other types so it hasn't been under as much pressure and heat.

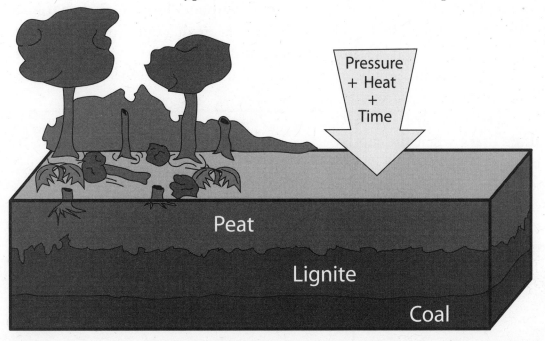

Pressure + Heat + Time

Peat

Lignite

Coal

49

Getting coal out of the ground is a dirty, dangerous business. There's always a risk of tunnels collapsing. Methane gas trapped within coal can explode when exposed to air, and it's toxic for the **miners** to breathe. Even the dust created from cutting into the coal can cause lung problems for the miners, called black lung disease.

LET'S FIND COAL...IF YOU DON'T "MINED"

The United States has a lot of coal deposits. It's found in almost every state. Much of the United States' coal is in the Appalachian region, mostly in West Virginia and Pennsylvania. There's another band of coal deposits in the middle of the United States, in states like Texas, Kansas, Missouri, and Illinois. In the west, Wyoming, Utah, and Arizona all have coal deposits. Wyoming is the state with the highest coal production in the United States.

> **Once the miners are down in the shafts, they start digging at the layers of coal, tumbling them onto conveyors that bring the coal up to the surface.**

Coal is located by either discovering **outcroppings** above the ground, or by drilling for samples underground. The drill cuts away a sample of the rocks below, and then the sample is brought back up to the surface. If coal is found in that sample, then coal mines are dug into the ground. First, vertical **shafts** are dug down into the ground, then horizontal shafts are dug out. Coal miners have to travel to the shafts on elevators or coal trains that run deep into the ground. Some coal deposits are right below the surface, but others are as deep as 1,000 feet (305 meters) below the ground.

We also get coal by **strip mining**. That's when the top layers of earth that cover the coal are ripped up or "stripped" away from the coal layers, using huge steam shovels.

Did you know?

For every person in the United States, a little under 4 tons of coal is used each year to generate electricity.

First, all the trees are bulldozed. Then they're dumped in a nearby area, along with any bushes, underbrush, and soil. Holes are drilled into the rock that lay just below the surface of the land. Explosives placed into those holes break up the rock into chunks. That rock is removed and dumped, too.

The goal is to expose the coal layer without blowing it into bits. Once the coal is reached, it's lifted out by heavy machinery in long strips. When the first strip is removed, the machines move onto the strip that's right beside it. Any **debris** is piled on top of the space left by the coal that was just removed. This continues until the whole area has been mined.

Words to Know

miner: person who works in a mine.

outcropping: piece of rock sticking up above the ground.

shaft: a tunnel or passage.

strip mining: the process of mining coal where the top layers of the earth are removed.

debris: the remains of something, such as dirt, rocks, and vegetation.

slurry: a mixture of coal and water, which allows coal to travel through pipelines.

Afterward, the land is pretty much destroyed—everything's been all dug up, turned over, or hauled away to be dumped elsewhere. Rainwater has nothing to soak into because all the soil has been removed. So it just runs off into streams, taking debris and dirt with it. This pollutes the water. To save the land, mining companies need to rebuild the mountain by bringing in soil, and replanting trees and plants. That hasn't always happened in the past because it costs a lot of money.

Coal is a non-renewable energy source.

Once the coal is extracted from the ground, it's shipped to its destinations by boats, trains, or pipelines (like natural gas). But solids don't flow like liquids or gases, so the coal has to be prepped for its trip down the pipeline. To do this, it's ground up and then mixed with water. The resulting fluid is called **slurry**, and it's pumped through the pipelines for miles. Once it reaches its destination, the slurry is filtered, removing the coal from the water—just like you can sift water and sand through a beach toy strainer.

Did you know?

Burning coal is the most common source of electricity in the United States. We use it to generate 50 percent of our electricity.

THE ADVANTAGES AND DISADVANTAGES OF COAL

Although coal is a popular energy source, there are positive and negative aspects to its use.

Some of the benefits are:
* We have lots of coal and it's readily available.
* It's a fairly cheap energy source.
* Coal is one of the most common sources of energy used to produce electricity today, so our current system to process it is well established.

Some of the disadvantages include:
* Coal is a non-renewable energy source.
* Coal mining is destructive to the landscape.
* Coal mining can be an unhealthy job for the miners.
* Burning coal contributes to greenhouse gases that pollute our atmosphere.

COAL CANDY

Make Your Own

Just for fun, and to use in the next activity, this recipe will give you a realistic-looking coal candy to share with your friends and family while you tell them about this fossil fuel.

! Caution: This project involves very hot liquids, so you need an adult to help.

supplies

- foil
- 8-inch-square baking pan
- cooking spray
- 2 cups sugar
- ¾ cup corn syrup
- ½ cup water
- heavy saucepan
- spoon for stirring
- candy thermometer
- 1 teaspoon anise extract
- black food coloring (paste works best if you have it)
- mallet or hammer

1. Line the bottom and sides of the baking pan with tin foil. Spray it lightly with cooking spray.

2. Mix the sugar, corn syrup, and water in the saucepan. Cook the mixture over medium heat, stirring contstantly. Stir gently so you don't get sugar up the sides of the pan.

3. When the sugar is dissolved completely and the mixture begins to boil, clip the candy thermometer carefully to the side of the pan. Be sure you don't let the bottom of the thermometer rest on the bottom of the pan.

4. Without stirring, keep cooking your mixture until the temperature of the liquid is 290 degrees Fahrenheit. Remove the pan from the heat and let it cool slightly. Stir in the anise extract and the food coloring.

5. Pour your mixture into the pan and let it cool completely. After it's cool, lift the candy out of the pan using the foil to help you. Set it on the counter and cover it with another layer of foil. Using the mallet or hammer, gently break the candy into small pieces—and you've got coal!

Make Your Own COAL LAYERS

Use the candy you made in the previous activity to create a realistic layer of land. With this project, you'll be able to see how the landscape formed over the years, and how coal is part of it all. Each layer in this edible project represents a different layer of the landscape, as it formed over time.

supplies

- flavored gelatin (lime, raspberry, and lemon)
- boiling water
- measuring cup
- clear glass pan
- fruit cocktail and sliced banana
- crushed graham crackers
- coal candy from the previous project
- ½ cup whipped cream or whipped topping

1. Make the lime gelatin according to the package directions, but using a little less water than the directions call for. Pour it into the glass pan, and place the pan in the refrigerator until it's completely set. Be sure you put the pan on the shelf so that it's nice and flat. This is your first layer, the layer of limestone.

2. The next layer is going to be sandstone, made with raspberry gelatin. Make the gelatin with the same directions you used for the limestone. Let this layer cool in the measuring cup for about 15 minutes.

3. After it's cooled for 15 minutes, add the banana pieces and fruit cocktail. The fruit cocktail should be well drained and patted dry with paper towels. These are the fossils that are often found in sandstone.

4. When you've mixed in your fossils, pour the whole thing over the first layer of limestone in your pan. Return the pan to the refrigerator and let it stay there until it's completely cool and firm.

5. Now comes the coal. Spread the crushed graham crackers mixed with chunks of coal candy over the layer of sandstone in the pan.

6. Make the lemon gelatin the same way you made the lime and raspberry gelatin, but just make half of it for this step. This is another layer of sandstone, but you can skip the fossils in this layer. Once you've made up half of the lemon, let it cool a little in the measuring cup, and then carefully pour it over your coal layer. Be sure to pour slowly so it doesn't stir up all the coal. Pop the pan back in the refrigerator again until it's cooled completely.

7. Mix up the remaining half of the lemon gelatin. Let it cool for about 15 minutes, and then mix in the whipped cream or whipped topping. This is going to be the siltstone layer—the final layer of landscape. Carefully spread this over the last layer of sandstone, and return it to the refrigerator one last time until it's set.

8. When your landscape is completely cooled, take it out and have a close look through the side of the pan. You can see how the layers of the earth have been deposited over time, including the layer of coal that was formed by the pressure of the layers above it.

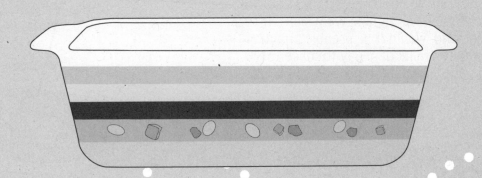

COAL MINING EXPERIMENT

How hard is it to pull out coal from the ground? What does mining do to the surrounding landscape? Find out with this (delicious) coal mining experiment.

1. Begin by evaluating the area you're going to mine, in this case, the chocolate chip cookies. The chocolate chips are your "coal" deposits, so that's what you're looking for. Without picking the cookies up (after all, real miners can't look under the ground first), consider the best place to begin mining.

2. Estimate how much "coal" you're going to be able to extract from your land. Real mining operations have to decide if it's going to be worth the cost of all their efforts to retrieve coal from an area of land.

3. Use your paper clip or toothpick tools to chip away at the cookies and dig out the "coal." As you extract each "coal" chunk, put it on your plate. As tempting as it may be to eat your "coal," wait until the end to see if your "coal" output equalled your estimates.

4. Once you've mined everything you can out of the cookies, examine what's left. If this were real land, would it be useable again? See if you can think of a way to make the mining have less of an impact on the land.

supplies

- chocolate chip cookies
- mining tools, like paper clips or toothpicks
- plate

Chapter 7
Nuclear Power

It's easy to see how wind or water can be sources of energy—if you've been toppled by a stiff wind or knocked over by a wave you know how strong those forces can be. But what about something you can't see? Something so small that you need a microscope to see it? Can something that small really be powerful enough to generate energy that we can use?

We're talking about atoms, and they really can be that powerful. Atoms are the tiny particles that make up every single thing in the entire universe that has matter. And you know that atoms are made of even tinier particles—neutrons, electrons, and protons. Here's what scientists discovered in 1919: If you split an atom, or break it apart, energy is released. They figured out how to harness that energy, and how to create it whenever they wanted.

Nuclear power is a non-renewable energy source.

The key is in a little particle called a neutron. Back in chapter three, you saw that hydrogen is the simplest element. Each atom of hydrogen has one proton and one electron. Hydrogen doesn't have any neutrons, but most other types of matter do have neutrons. Neutrons are the particles that have no charge at all (remember, protons have a positive charge, and electrons have a negative charge). Some atoms have more than one neutron, and some atoms have lots. The element **uranium** has between 141 and 146 neutrons.

URANIUM

Because it's so unstable and easy to split apart, uranium is used as the fuel source for nuclear power. The element uranium is found in a mineral called uranium ore. It's dug out of the ground from large deposits in places like the United States and Canada.

If an element can change easily into something else, it's called "unstable." When that unstable element **decays**, it breaks apart, or changes. Different elements are either stable or unstable. Hydrogen is an element that is considered stable, because it doesn't change very easily at all. An element like uranium, though, is considered very unstable, because it's easy to break it open.

Compare cracking open an egg to cracking open a bowling ball. The egg is easier to break open—it's more unstable. The bowling ball is really tough to break open, because it's very stable.

If uranium is hit by a neutron, it splits open. It decays. Uranium's nucleus, where the protons and neutrons are, disintegrates and **radiates** energy. Some of that energy is in the form of waves of energy similar to **x-rays**. This is called **radiation**. Because of its intense energy, radiation can harm or even destroy living cells. It's very dangerous to humans and other living organisms.

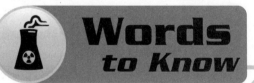

Words to Know

uranium: the element used as fuel in nuclear reactions.

decay: when an atom breaks down.

radiate: when energy spreads or extends away from a source.

x-ray: radiation that allows doctors to see your bones.

radiation: when energy moves away from the source in waves.

GOIN' FISSION

So how is the energy created? Scientists discovered that if they shot a neutron at an atom of uranium, the uranium atom would break open, releasing energy—and more neutrons. If the scientists controlled the reaction and slowed it down, one released neutron would strike another uranium atom. That atom would release more energy and neutrons, and one of the neutrons would hit another uranium atom, and so on. This **controlled chain reaction** is how energy is generated in a nuclear power plant. The entire process—uranium atoms being split by neutrons from other decaying atoms and releasing energy—is called **fission**.

Words to Know

controlled chain reaction: when a nuclear reaction is controlled, allowing only one neutron to continue on from a split atom to hit a new atom.

fission: the nuclear reaction where a neutron splits an atom, releasing heat energy and more neutrons.

uncontrolled chain reaction: when the splitting of atoms and the release of energy and neutrons is magnified and grows rapidly.

To understand a chain reaction better, picture a line of kids, each holding one Easter egg with malt balls inside. Now imagine one more person arrives and hands the first girl in line one more malt ball. The girl opens her Easter egg, takes out a malt ball, and gives it to the next person in line. Then that person opens their egg, and passes a malt ball to the next person, and so on. That's a controlled chain reaction.

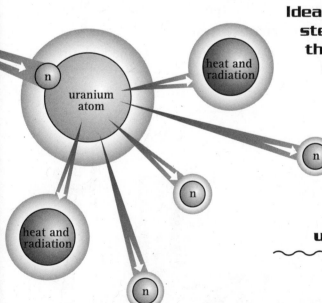

Ideally, nuclear reactions are all steady and slow. But when more than one neutron from the decaying atom hits more than one uranium atom, that sets off a much bigger and more powerful chain reaction. When many neutrons are splitting many other atoms, which are releasing more neutrons that hit and split many other atoms, it is called an **uncontrolled chain reaction.**

MELTING DOWN

One of the dangers of using nuclear power is the risk of radiation to living things. While most of the risk may come from a slow leak of radiation, another risk can be a larger disaster called a **meltdown**. While the process of fission is a controlled chain reaction, if the reaction pattern becomes uncontrolled, it can result in a destructive nuclear explosion releasing massive amounts of radiation. That's what happened in 1986 in a Ukrainian city called Chernobyl in the worst nuclear accident in history. A nuclear explosion at the plant spread radioactive materials into the environment.

Back to our Easter eggs, suppose the person arriving hands a malt ball to the first person, who opens her egg and gives *two* people malt balls. Those two people each open their eggs and each pass out two new malt balls. Now six people are involved (the original two, plus the four who are now involved). So, those four new people would each open their eggs and pass on two malt balls to two new people—getting *eight* new people involved, and so on. The chain reaction is much, much bigger and grows much quicker.

When you're passing out malt balls, it may seem that faster is better—especially if you like malt balls. But when an uncontrolled chain reaction happens in nuclear energy, the release of power is too great to control. In 1945, there was an experiment called the Manhattan Project, named after the location in New York where the research began. In this project, scientists tested the first nuclear weapon in the desert of New Mexico. The process was an uncontrolled chain reaction, and it created an incredibly powerful blast that was extremely destructive—and very deadly.

NUCLEAR REACTORS

Nuclear power plants are similar to traditional power plants. They both heat water to create steam, which drives a turbine generator to generate electricity. The difference between them is how they heat that water. Traditional plants may burn coal or natural gas to create heat to boil the water. That process uses fossil fuels.

Nuclear plants use the heat that's generated by fission to heat the water.

But how do you contain nuclear fission, to prevent any radiation from leaking out into the environment? Scientists and engineers are very careful! They build nuclear power plants to very tight safety specifications to keep them safe.

The **nuclear reactor** is the place in the power plant where the nuclear reactions take place. The reaction is carefully managed to create the desired controlled chain reaction. One of the ways the nuclear reaction rate is slowed down is by using **control rods**.

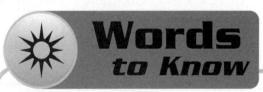

Words to Know

meltdown: an uncontrolled reaction in a nuclear power plant.

nuclear reactor: the place where a nuclear reaction takes place in a nuclear power plant.

control rods: devices to absorb neutrons.

moderator: a substance that slows the rate of a nuclear reaction in the power plant by keeping it cool.

These metal rods, made out of special materials, absorb the extra neutrons that are released when atoms are split. This keeps them from splitting other atoms and causing an uncontrolled chain reaction.

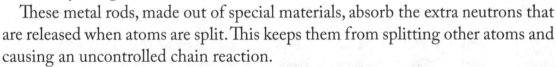

Something else that helps slow the reaction down is a **moderator**. Usually water or carbon, the moderator flows upward between the control rods, cooling them down and slowing down the process of atom splitting. Molecules move at different speeds—when they're hot, they move faster. That's how food cooks. But when they're cold, they move slower. Keeping the reaction cooler helps slow it down.

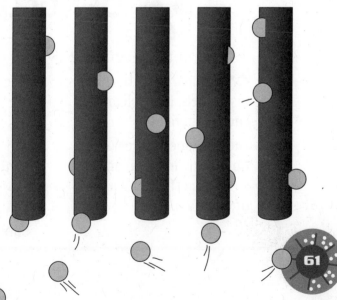

The entire core of the plant—the place where the nuclear reaction takes place—is protected by very thick layers of concrete. The job of the concrete is to absorb the radiation and protect the environment if there's a leak. So, there's a whole lot of precautions taken to protect us all from dangerous, uncontrolled reactions and radiation.

Did you know?

Nuclear submarines are huge—sometimes as long as two football fields!

POWER UP

As the water is heated from nuclear fission, it flows to another part of the plant, where it boils and produces steam to drive the turbine, just like in other plants. The turbine generates electricity.

But there's another use for nuclear power, and it's located under the water. Nuclear submarines are fueled by the energy produced in nuclear reactors they carry on board. The benefit of a nuclear-powered submarine is that it can stay out at sea for months without having to come back to refuel with fossil fuels.

Nuclear power generates about 19 percent of the electricity used in the United States.

ADVANTAGES AND DISADVANTAGES OF NUCLEAR POWER

Some of the benefits are:

❖ Compared to burning fossil fuels, it's a cleaner energy source.

❖ The fuel doesn't get used up quickly in the reactor, so it's an efficient source of energy.

Some of the disadvantages include:

❖ Nuclear power is non-renewable. Uranium ore still needs to be mined from the earth.

❖ It can be dangerous. If radiation leaks, it can be deadly. If the reaction gets out of control, the process can be explosive.

❖ The leftover nuclear material that isn't converted to energy is difficult and dangerous to dispose of.

CHAIN REACTION BOWLING SET

Make Your Own

supplies

- 20 paper cups
- modeling clay
- duct tape
- tennis ball
- ruler

1. Stick a small lump of modeling clay on the inside bottom of 10 paper cups. For each "pin," invert one empty cup over the cup with modeling clay and tape it securely, rim to rim.

2. Set up the 10 pins in a traditional bowling pattern. One goes in the first row, two in the next row, three in the next, and four in the last row. Space your pins far enough apart that they're not touching each other, but close enough that when they fall, they hit each other.

3. Shape some modeling clay into a ball or use a tennis ball. Roll your ball toward the pins, aiming for the first (solo) pin. Watch the other pins carefully. If you hit it right, the first will knock the second two, then each of those will knock into more in the next row, and so on. This is essentially what an uncontrolled chain reaction is like in nuclear fission.

4. Set the pins back up. Now take the ruler and have someone hold it diagonally between the pins. You want to divide the pins into two sections so the solo pin and the three pins behind it running down one side are separate from the rest.

5. Roll the ball again. This time, when you hit the lead pin, that pin will hit the second, and the second will hit the third. This is the same as a controlled chain reaction—the desired response in a nuclear power plant!

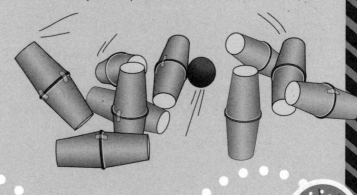

63

Chapter 8
Wind Power

When you think of wind, you may think of a breeze that lifts your kite or that makes a paper windmill spin. But can the wind generate enough power to supply electricity to hundreds of homes?

It sure can. If you've ever doubted the power of the wind, consider a hurricane or tornado. The winds that these storms whip up can demolish buildings and rip trees right out of the ground. So the wind can really be a potent energy source.

Wind energy has been harnessed for thousands of years to perform useful work for humans.

BLOWIN' IN THE WIND

Wind is just moving air. It's created by the sun's energy. The earth is made up of different types of surfaces—dark forests, sunny deserts, and huge bodies of water, for example. When the sun warms the land and the air over it, the warm air expands and rises. If there's cooler air nearby, over a different kind of surface like an ocean, that cooler air will rush in to fill the space left by the rising warm air. That's when you feel the air move, which is wind.

Did you know?

One-third of America's electricity could be produced by the wind in the state of North Dakota alone!

If we used wind power to generate electricity for our homes, you wouldn't have to get your own wind turbine in your yard. Instead, wind power plants called **wind farms** would convert the wind's power into electricity. Then the electricity would come to your house, just like it does today.

HARNESSING WIND

Capturing the power of the wind for energy is nothing new. As far back as the ancient Egyptians, people have used wind-powered sailing ships to travel. Early civilizations used wind-powered mills to grind their grain or pump water.

Today's windmills aren't just for grinding grain any more—they can generate electricity for our power-hungry civilizations. Wind machines are called **turbines**, and their job is to capture the wind's kinetic energy. The turbines sit on a tall, skinny structure usually made out of aluminum or steel.

How does it work? There are blades on the turbine that are shaped to create **drag** against the wind. These blades spin at about 10 to 50 turns per minute. They're connected to a drive shaft, and as the wind flows over these blades, they spin and make the drive shaft turn an electric generator. The generator transforms the wind's kinetic energy into electrical energy.

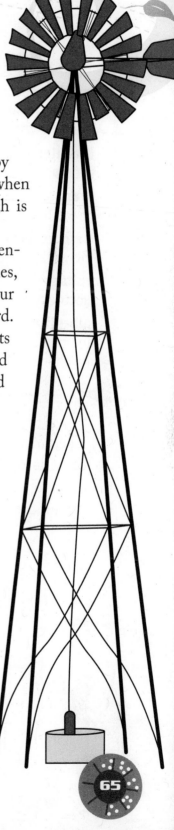

Words to Know

wind farm: a group of wind machines that generate electricity from the wind.

turbine: wind machine that converts wind power to electricity.

drag: a force that slows down or resists the wind.

transformer: a device that changes the voltage of electricity.

voltage: the amount of force in the electricity.

substation: between the power plant and homes, where electricity is reduced in voltage.

This electricity then passes through cables to a **transformer** that zaps the **voltage** up higher. The transformer does this by changing the magnetic field, kind of like the generator did, to create a higher charge. That's because the electricity has to be at a high voltage to make the journey for hundreds of miles from the power plant to your home.

In the next leg of the journey the electricity passes through more cables to **substations**, where the voltage is brought back down to a lower level and passed along to homes. The voltage has to be reduced, or else it will be too high for the electronics in your house to handle.

Wind turbines do best with an average wind speed of 10 miles (16 kilometers) per hour or more. A good location for them is along the coast of an ocean or lake, since the strongest winds usually blow from water onto land. Mountaintops or wide open flat areas are other good locations. They also need to be located close to where the energy will be used, because it is less efficient to send electricity hundreds of miles away from where it's generated.

Did you know?

If they put a wind farm in Antarctica, it would be very busy—Antarctica has average winds of 40 miles (65 kilometers) per hour. Getting the power generated there to those who need it might be tricky, though . . .

Did you know?

The largest wind turbine in the world is being built in Germany. From the tip of one blade to the tip of another is over 400 feet (122 meters)! It could power almost 2,000 homes in America for the whole year—all by itself!

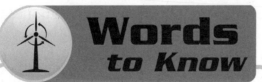

Words to Know

meteorological: involving the weather and climate.

anemometer: an instrument used to measure the wind. The number of times it spins is calculated and converted into miles per hour.

power grid: the network of cables that transport electricity all over the country.

Turbines are positioned high up in the air because that's where the winds are steadiest. Winds are also stronger up high, because they aren't slowed down by the drag of the land or structures.

Before turbines are set up, people study an area and test the wind to make sure the conditions are right for a turbine. They study wind maps, use **meteorological** data, and measure winds using an instrument called an **anemometer**.

Wind is a renewable energy source.

APPLES, CORN...AND WIND?

You're probably used to farms harvesting your usual lineup of crops like apples, corn, and wheat. But there are wind farms that have anywhere from a handful to over 100 turbines to harvest wind. The turbines are linked together so they can channel all their combined energy to produce a larger electrical output.

Wind farms are a good way to use land, too, because the land itself can still be used for agriculture. The largest wind farm so far is in Texas, with 421 turbines at work.

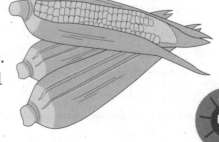

The United States generates enough wind power to supply electricity to almost 7 million households every year. This might sound like a lot but it's only about 1 percent of the electricity our country uses.

Some of the windiest places in the country are perfect for wind farms, but they're not located very close to major cities. The Midwest is flat and wide open for hundreds and hundreds of miles. Most of the Midwest is quite rural, though. Transporting wind-generated electricity long distances is difficult. Right now, most power lines run from power plants located close to cities. So more transmission lines will need to be laid between remote wind farm locations and the places that need most of the power.

Offshore wind farms may seem like a good idea because it's so windy at the ocean. But it's more expensive to install turbines out at sea than putting them on land. Plus, you have the same problems in establishing new transmission lines from way out in the ocean to homes. Although wind power is a growing source of electricity, it definitely has a few road bumps left to navigate.

ADVANTAGES AND DISADVANTAGES OF WIND POWER

Wind power is gaining in popularity in the United States.

Some of its advantages are:

- It's free and renewable. There will always be patterns of wind around the planet, and you can't use it up.
- The land used for a wind farm can still be used for other things, such as growing corn and wheat.
- Generating electricity from wind doesn't produce the greenhouse gases or other pollutants that come from fossil fuels or nuclear fission.
- A home that is far away from the **power grid** can generate its own electricity with wind.

But capturing and using wind power does have drawbacks, too. Here are some disadvantages of wind power:

- It isn't always windy enough.
- Some people find the turbines unattractive, especially when they're along a scenic ocean coast.
- Turbines can be noisy—some sound like a speeding car!
- When wind speeds vary, the amount of electricity produced varies. It's not always a steady source.

HOVERCRAFT

Make Your Own

Wind doesn't have to be a powerful force to produce energy. With this simple hovercraft, you can see how even a gentle wind can move a vehicle.

supplies

- sports cap from a drink bottle
- CD
- glue
- balloon

1. Glue the sports cap to the top of the CD, directly over the hole in the CD. Close the cap.

2. Blow up the balloon, and pinch it shut as far up the neck as you can. Stretch the remaining long neck of the balloon over the cap.

3. Pinching through the balloon neck, open the sports cap and give the hovercraft a gentle push.

4. As the air blows through the hole in the CD, the hovercraft will "float" across the table's surface.

Did you know?

The strongest wind ever recorded on Earth was in 1934. A gust of wind blasted across the top of Mount Washington in New Hampshire at 231 miles per hour.

ANEMOMETER

What's the wind like where you live? A gentle breeze—or powerful gusts? Find out with this anemometer. You'll be able to see proof of how strong or weak the wind is in your own backyard.

supplies

- scissors
- 4 paper cups
- markers or paint in one or more colors
- thick corrugated cardboard box
- stapler
- thin nail
- hammer
- thick wooden dowel

1. Cut the rims off the paper cups. This will make them lighter and easier to turn. Paint one of the cups, leaving the others plain. Or, you can paint three one color and the fourth another color.

2. Cut two strips about 20 inches long and 3 inches wide from the cardboard box. Put the strips down, and position the cups so each one is at one end of a cardboard strip. For each pair of cups, position them so one open end is facing one direction, and the other cup is facing in the opposite direction.

3. Lay the cardboard over the cups and attach each cup with the stapler. You should now have two cardboard strips, each with a cup on both ends—be sure the cups are facing in opposite directions.

4. Position the strips so they form an X. Try to make it as even as possible so the cups are all the same distance from the center. Hammer the nail through the two cardboard strips into the top of the dowel.

5. Turn the cardboard X a few times to loosen up the nail hole and allow your cups to spin freely. Test it by blowing into the cups.

6. Take your anemometer outside and stick the dowel into the ground. Your anemometer will spin in the breeze. Use the colored cup as a gauge to count how many times your instrument spins per minute. If you check it on different days you'll start to understand wind in terms of your own anemometer.

WIND-POWERED INSTRUMENT

Make Your Own

The wind can do more than create power. It can also make music! Wind chimes are a traditional way to make music, but this wind-powered instrument will add some new sounds to the garden. Have an adult help you with the wire cutters.

supplies

- your anemometer from the previous project
- scissors
- soft plastic container top
- glue and duct tape
- shoebox
- thin wire or rubber bands
- wire cutters or thumb tacks
- dowel

1. Cut a piece of plastic from the container top into a shape like a guitar pick. Using glue or tape, attach the pick to one of the cups on your anemometer so it sticks out past the edge of the cup.

2. Tape the lid of the shoebox firmly in place. Using the scissors, cut a hole about 2 or 3 inches square in the center of one wide side of the shoebox.

3. If you're using wire, cut four pieces about 2 inches longer than the size of your hole. Tape them across the hole in the shoebox. It should look a little like a guitar.

4. If you're using rubber bands, stretch them tightly across the hole and secure them with tape or around thumbtacks. You can also stretch the rubber bands right around the box.

5. You want to align the instrument with the anemometer so that the pick hits the strings as the wind blows the anemometer around. Using the duct tape, secure your shoebox guitar instrument to its own dowel.

6. Once you find the right position, stick the dowel attached to the instrument into the ground. When the wind blows, you'll have a wind-powered guitar for your garden!

Chapter 9
Hydropower

Have you ever been swimming in the ocean, and been hit by a wave that sent you tumbling head over heels? Then you know how powerful water can be. Water has the power to sweep away buildings in a flood or change the landscape through **erosion**. So it's no surprise that people have been harnessing water power for thousands of years.

Hydropower is a renewable energy source.

The Greek word "hydro" means water, so **hydropower** means using water for power. Ancient civilizations harnessed water power to **irrigate** their crops and grind grain.

Later, water was used to power saws to cut lumber. Water can be blasted at high power to remove rocks and gems from their surroundings, in a process called **hydraulic** mining. The energy from the flowing ocean tides can be captured, as can power from the movement of waves.

WATER WHEELS

Water wheels have been powering civilizations for thousands of years. You need a moving water source to make them work, so places along rivers are perfect locations for them. There are two kinds of water wheels. With an overshot wheel, the water is poured over the top of the wheel. The other kind is called an undershot. With this type, the wheel is set into flowing water. As the water pushes past the wheel, it turns the wheel. Either way, the power of the turning wheel turned gears that worked the mill stones that ground grain.

HOW IT WORKS

So how is electricity created from hydropower? Electricity produced through water power is called **hydroelectricity**. It's most often created with **dams**. Dams are large, strong walls that hold back water, often in a river. The walls create a standing water source—a lake. The flowing water from the lake can be controlled and its power captured as it falls. Sometimes the water falls hundreds of feet.

Words to Know

erosion: when land is worn away by water flow.

hydropower: power from water.

irrigate: moving water from one area to another to water crops.

hydraulic: using water to operate or move something.

water wheel: a large wheel with buckets or paddles that move as water flows through it.

hydroelectricity: electricity produced by water power.

dam: a large, strong wall that holds back water.

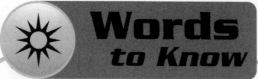

Words to Know

reservoir: a body of water that's stored for future energy use. It can be natural or man-made.

evaporate: when a liquid heats up and changes into a gas.

radiate: to spread outward.

condense: when water cools down, it changes from a gas (water vapor) back into a liquid (water).

tide: the daily rising and falling of ocean water, based on the pull of the moon's and sun's gravity.

First, a large area of land or an existing body of water is designated as the future water source. The dam holds back the water so the land is flooded, creating a lake called a **reservoir**. This water is potential energy for future electricity.

Then as the dam slowly releases the water from the reservoir, the water is pulled by gravity down through the dam toward the river below it. One of the things that determines the amount of electricity generated is the height of the dam. The higher the dam, the farther the water falls and the more power it has.

The water falls through a turbine, spinning the turbine's blades. In the same way that other energy sources generate electricity, the spinning turbine turns a shaft connected to a generator. The generator convents that mechanical energy into electricity. Finally, transmission lines carry the electricity from the hydroelectric power plant to its destination—homes and businesses.

The generator converts the energy into electric energy in a way similar to how it's converted in a wind turbine. The moving water makes the turbine turn.

IT'S GETTING STEAMY

Just as liquid water can be used as an energy source, so can water in another form: steam. When water is heated to 212 degrees Fahrenheit (100 degrees Celsius), it starts to boil. And when it's boiling, the liquid water gradually **evaporates**, changing to a gas. This gas is called water vapor, or steam.

THE HOOVER DAM

Completed in 1936, the Hoover Dam is one of the largest dams in the world. Standing on the edge of the dam, where a road crosses between Arizona and Nevada, you can look over the side and see the Colorado River over 700 feet below. The building of the dam created Lake Mead, a huge reservoir in the middle of the desert, where people waterski, swim, and lounge in the sun. The Hoover Dam contains enough concrete to pave a highway from Maine to California. Electricity generated by the hydropower of the dam provides nearly all the power for Las Vegas, and powers other cities and towns from Arizona to Los Angeles.

The construction of the Hoover Dam cost $49 million! That's equal to $736 million today. But it cost more than just money. During the five years it took to build the dam, 112 workers died. It is such a large and impressive dam that it was named a National Monument in 1985.

A steam system can provide heat energy to a home, using boiling water to generate steam, which fills pipes. The hot pipes then **radiate** heat throughout the house. This can also be accomplished using hot water in the pipes instead of steam. You still need to burn something to heat the water in the first place, though, like oil.

Steam is used in a steam engine to provide mechanical energy to drive a generator. At the end of the process, the steam **condenses** back into water, and the cycle can start all over again.

Steam shows how hydropower is renewable. Once that steam is made, you're putting that water back into the environment in the form of water vapor. Eventually it will become available again as liquid water.

Did you know?

More than 2,000 years ago, the ancient Greeks used water power to grind wheat into flour.

ENERGY

IN THE TIDES

Have you ever visited the beach one day, and enjoyed a huge expanse of sand to build sand-castles on? Then you returned the very next day, only to find that the huge beach had somehow shrunk into a narrow stretch of sand? Did the ocean suddenly move closer, gobbling up the shoreline?

In a way, it did. What you experienced was a low **tide** (the first day), where the ocean's waters were farther away from shore. The second day, you were there at high tide. The waters were much higher, creeping up over the beach.

Did you know?

The largest producer of hydropower in the world is Canada, followed by the United States.

Tides are formed by the pull of gravity from the moon and the sun. That gravitational force makes the oceans of the earth bulge, sometimes being "high" and strong, and other times being "low." When the tides are strong, so is the tidal power.

Remember how the wind can change in a moment and is unpredictable? Tides are predictable and regular. Tides are based on the changing positions of the moon, sun, and earth. The earth's daily rotation is also part of it. Think about a glass of water. While you're holding it, if you move back and forth, the water in the glass moves, too. That's sort of like the oceans on the earth—they shift and change based on the tugs and pulls from the forces of gravity and the spinning earth.

Harnessing the power of the tides is another way water can be used to generate energy for humans to use. Tidal power can be used by capturing the water during a high tide, and when it "ebbs," or flows back out to the sea, that movement generates energy that can be used. Tide stream generators use the force of the moving water to power generators. They're almost like windmills for the water.

WAVE!

While tidal power captures the energy created by the movement of the tides, wave power can also be used. Waves are created when wind blows across the surface of the water. There's motion energy created on the surface of the water by the waves as they rise and fall. Spend a day at the beach when there's some surf and you'll notice how much energy waves hold.

There are a couple of ways to capture wave power. One uses floats or buoys—things that can bob on the surface of the water. They generate electricity because as the water rises and falls, the floats can drive a pump system. Another way is with devices that use the rise and fall of water to move water up and down inside a cylindrical shaft. So far, wave power hasn't been used very much. This is partly because waves can vary a lot from day to day. Sometimes the power of the waves can be incredible but other times the ocean can be calm.

THE ADVANTAGES AND DISADVANTAGES OF HYDROPOWER

Hydropower has a lot of benefits:

- Hydropower is a renewable energy source.
- The water in a lake or reservoir can be used for other purposes too, like recreation or irrigation.
- Water doesn't have to be used immediately. It can be stored in the reservoir for later.
- Dams are sturdy enough to last for a very long time.
- Dams and the electricity produced by hydropower don't contribute carbon dioxide or other greenhouse gases to the atmosphere. They don't create any waste product.

But the drawbacks include:

- Dams are very expensive to build.
- Dams are destructive to the local environment because they change it.
- When dams are built, people who live in the areas that will be flooded must move.
- If something goes wrong and a dam breaks, the flooding can be devastating. Fortunately, modern engineering reduces the chances of this happening.
- If the dams block the path of fish who travel upstream to lay eggs, they can be unable to reproduce.

WATER TURBINE

Isaac Newton was a famous scientist who made important discoveries about how things work. He found that for every action there is an equal and opposite reaction. This is called Newton's Third Law of Motion. See Isaac Newton's idea in action with this simple water turbine. When water pours out of one of the holes, its force makes the carton rotate in the opposite direction. The more holes you poke in your turbine, the faster it will spin.

supplies

- hammer and nail
- milk carton
- duct tape
- string
- water

1. Using the hammer and nail, poke a hole on the side of the milk carton, about an inch from the bottom and an inch from the right side.

2. Poke another hole on the very next side of the milk carton, in the same location—about an inch from the bottom and an inch from the right side. Repeat this on the other two sides. Cover all of the holes with duct tape. Poke one last hole on the top of the milk carton, and tie a long string through it.

3. Your turbine is ready to go! Fill it with water, and take it outside. Hang your turbine from a low tree branch or another place that lets it hang freely.

4. Take the tape off of one hole. The turbine will start to spin as the water is forced out through the hole.

5. Try taking the tape off the hole on the side opposite of the open one. Then try taking all four pieces of tape off. Your turbine's power will increase as the holes are opened—as long as you keep adding more water when it runs out, that is!

WATER WHEEL

Make Your Own

Experiment with the strength of water power with your own water wheel.

1. Make eight cuts in your pie plate and fold back the flaps as shown in the diagram (cut along the solid lines and fold back along the dotted lines). Be sure you don't cut all the way to the center of the plate!

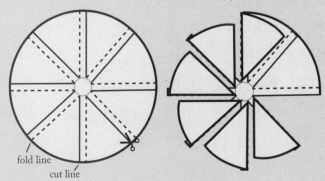

fold line

cut line

2. Poke a hole in the very center of the plate and push the straw through. It should be a very snug fit. If you need to, tape the straw to the pie plate. Insert the skewer or thin pencil through the straw. If you can't hold both ends of the skewer, snip the straw a little on both ends so you can hold it. The wheel should be able to spin freely when you hold the skewer.

3. Tie one end of the string to one end of the straw. Attach the weight to the other end of the string. Trim the string so the weight is hanging about 10 inches past the wheel.

4. Your water wheel is finished. Turn on the water and hold the water wheel by both ends of the skewer under the flow. Your wheel should turn and lift the weight. Experiment with different water flows and different weights to see how strong the water can be.

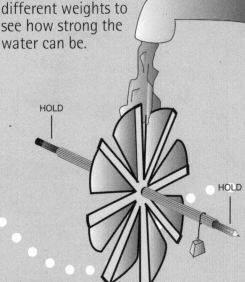

HOLD

HOLD

supplies

- aluminum pie plate
- scissors
- straw
- tape
- skewer or pencil
- 2-foot-long string
- small weights such as a fishing sinker and stones
- faucet or other running water source

Chapter 10

Solar Power

There's nothing in the universe that quite matches the sun as a power generator. Every single second, the sun cranks out 40,000,000,000,000,000,000,000,000 **joules** of energy. For comparison, a 100-watt lightbulb only uses 100 joules per second. The sun is an energy-producing powerhouse like nothing else in our solar system.

Solar power is a renewable energy source.

Constantly, the sun sends light and heat energy to Earth that's used by all living creatures. The sun's energy also warms the water, land, and air—and you've already seen how that creates wind.

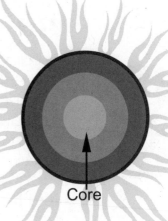

Core

BUT WHERE DOES IT COME FROM?

The sun generates its own energy. Because it's made of gases called helium and hydrogen, the sun isn't solid like the earth. At the very center—the core—of the sun, hydrogen atoms are flung around because of the high heat.

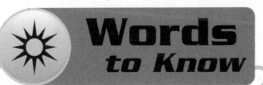

Words to Know

joule: a unit of electrical energy.

fuse: to join together under high heat by melting.

nuclear fusion: the process of hydrogen converting to helium and releasing energy.

When those atoms bump into each other, the hydrogen is **fused**, or transformed into helium. This process is called **nuclear fusion**, and when this happens, heat and light energy are released. That energy travels through space—and a small amount of it reaches Earth.

Only a fraction of the energy that hits the earth reaches the ground, though. The rest stays in our atmosphere or is reflected back into space. But what does get to the surface is enough to warm the planet and produce solar energy that humans can harness to use for power.

SOLAR POWER IN THE PAST

Ancient Greeks built their homes facing south so the winter sun would shine inside and warm them. Some Native Americans built their homes in cliffs sides facing south for the same reason. It was common to heat water by setting water-filled barrels painted black out in the sun. The sun would heat the barrels to provide hot water later.

Did you know?

According to legend, an ancient Greek scientist named Archimedes used the power of the sun in a battle with the Romans. He set Roman ships on fire by reflecting sunlight into a fine point onto their ships. It created such heat they caught on fire.

SOLAR POWER TODAY

Today's solar-powered homes use the sun's energy to make the electricity they need. They use **solar cells** to collect the sun's energy. Solar cells that transform the sun's solar energy into electricity are called **photovoltaic cells** (PV cells). PV cells look like really flat sandwiches. They're made of special materials that absorb light. As they absorb the light, these materials also **conduct** some of the light's electrons away.

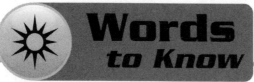

solar cells: devices used to capture the sun's radiant energy.

photovoltaic cells: solar cells that transform solar energy into electricity.

conduct: to transfer something.

passive solar: solar heat that's created without equipment.

This movement, or flow, of electrons is an electric current, like a microscopic river of electricity. When the PV cells have metal touching them, they can conduct the electricity away from the cell to the place that is receiving the electricity—for example, a solar house or car.

A group of PV cells is called an array. And a group of arrays together is called an array field. To power something large, a PV system will have several array fields. Small PV cells power everything from wrist watches to calculators.

TYPES OF SOLAR POWER

There are different types of solar power, too. If you've ever jumped in a car that's been sitting in the sun for a couple of hours on a summer day, you know pretty quickly that solar power's been at work. Your car is stuffy and hot, hot, hot! That's because of **passive solar** heating. Another example is when the water in a pond or in the ocean feels warmer at the end of the summer than at the beginning. If your house is positioned so that big windows face the morning sun, the house is just getting warmed up from the direct sunshine, with nothing mechanical to influence it. Early uses of solar power were all passive solar.

Technology gives us another form of solar power—an active system. That's when a collector gathers up the radiation and the heat is distributed through the use of fans or pumps. Collectors are shaped like giant satellite dishes or huge, curved troughs, with very shiny surfaces to redirect that energy. These types of devices turn to follow the sun all day.

If you can collect enough of the sun's rays, you can use that radiation energy to heat a fluid and produce steam. You've seen how steam can power generators. Steam can convert into mechanical energy with a turbine, which in turn moves a generator. And the generator creates electricity.

THE ADVANTAGES AND DISADVANTAGES OF SOLAR POWER

The sun is a star and stars don't last forever. But our sun still has a very long life left—billions of years.

The advantages of solar power are:

* Solar power is constantly renewing itself. It's a renewable energy source.
* Solar cells don't make any noise while they're collecting energy.
* There's no pollution created. It's clean energy.

The disadvantages of solar power are:

* Solar power is still expensive to generate. Converting an existing home to solar power is far more expensive than building a new solar home.
* You can't generate solar power at night.
* Solar power is limited on cloudy or rainy days. Some parts of the country don't get enough sunshine to make solar power a good choice.

Make Your Own SOLAR LASER

You can focus the sun's energy to melt an ice cube with this experiment. Be very careful when doing this project, though—have an adult watching and make sure you're not near anything flammable.

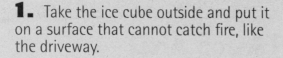

supplies

- magnifying glass
- ice cube
- sunny day

1. Take the ice cube outside and put it on a surface that cannot catch fire, like the driveway.

2. Locate the sun, and position your magnifying glass so that the sun's rays shine through it onto the ice cube. You may need to adjust the angle of your magnifying glass to make a very fine point of sunlight.

3. Once you've created a fine point, pick one spot on the ice cube, and focus the light on that one place. Don't move around too much.

4. The sun will begin to burn through the ice cube in a hole that goes straight through the cube.

Did you know?

In the 1830s, British astronomer John Herschel used solar energy to cook food during an expedition to Africa.

SOLAR S'MORES

Make Your Own

S'mores without a campfire? Sure! With the sun's help it's possible. For best results, wait for a warm day when it's at least 80 degrees out to try this.

supplies

- black construction paper or fabric
- clear glass baking dish with clear lid
- graham crackers
- chocolate bars
- mini marshmallows

1. Place the black paper outside in direct sunlight. Black will absorb the heat. Find a place that will be undisturbed and directly in the sun for a couple of hours. Make sure your dog and other critters don't have access to it!

2. Set the baking dish on top of the paper. Lay the graham crackers on the bottom of the baking dish.

3. Put chocolate bars on top of half of the graham crackers. Put the mini marshmallows on top of the other half of the graham crackers.

4. Cover the dish with the clear glass top and let the sun get to work. Keep checking back. When the marshmallows and chocolate are soft and melted, combine the halves to form s'mores.

Did you know?

Every hour, enough sunlight falls on the earth's surface to provide for the entire world's energy demands for an entire *year*.

85

Make Your Own

SOLAR WATER HEATER

You can heat water by setting it on the stove and using gas or electricity, or by putting it over a fire. Another way is to go straight to the most powerful source of energy there is—the sun. Here's how to make a simple solar water heater. Be careful though! The can and the water will get hot!

supplies

- empty soda can
- black paint and paintbrush
- tall deli container with a clear lid or a shoebox with plastic wrap as the lid
- water
- thermometer
- hammer and nail
- sunny day

1. Paint the soda can and the inside of the container or shoebox black. Let the paint dry.

2. Fill the can with water. Insert the thermometer into the water and record the temperature.

3. Using the hammer and nail, poke a hole in the cover of your container. If you are using a shoebox with plastic wrap, use the nail to poke a hole in the plastic. Position the can inside the container or box so when you put the top or plastic wrap on, you can put the thermometer through the hole.

4. Set your water heater out into the sun. About every 15 minutes, come back to check on the temperature.

5. You may wonder why putting the can in a container is even necessary. The container or shoe box acts as insulation. The sun heats up the air in the box, and that hot air insulates the can, raising the temperature higher, faster.

Chapter 11

Geothermal Energy

Thousands of miles below your feet, the earth is a boiling, **molten** mass of metals. No one knows the exact temperature of the center of the earth, but estimates are that it is 7,000 degrees Fahrenheit (3,871 degrees Celsius). What that means, besides being unimaginably hot, is that our planet contains heat energy that we can use for our needs.

> The Greek word *geo* means earth, and *therme* means heat.

The earth's heat is called **geothermal energy.** It's formed in the core of the earth. The very innermost part of the earth's core is thought to be made of solid metals. Surrounding that are the same metals, but they're molten—incredibly hot. That heat radiates outward through the next layer of the planet, which is called the mantle. The mantle is solid rock. The outermost layer of the earth is called the crust, and that's the part we live on, the part that's made of oceans and continents.

Crust

Mantle

Outer Core

Inner Core

The heat that radiates outward from the core gets released through the crust in different ways. Explosive volcanoes are one dramatic example. But volcanoes are so powerful and un-predictable that it's almost impossible for humans to harness the geothermal energy of a volcano. Not many people want to mess around with **lava** that can be 2,300 degrees Fahrenheit (1,260 degrees Celsius)! Fortunately, there are other ways the earth's heat is released that are a little less dangerous. It's through those outlets that humans can capture the heat energy to convert it to electricity.

Geothermal is a renewable energy source.

One of those outlets is through hot water. Water that comes from deep underground is heated by geo-thermal energy. It can come to the earth's surface as either hot water or steam. As you know, when water is heated enough, it eventually evaporates, turning into water vapor.

MOUNT SAINT HELENS

Until 1980, Mount Saint Helens was a large, steep mountain in Washington State that came to a pointed peak. Then a massive volcanic explosion occurred, so large that it blew the top right off of Mount Saint Helens. The height of the mountain went from 9,677 feet high to only 8,363 feet!

The eruption was deadly and disastrous. Ash spewed out across the United States, covering roads, roofs, and trees all the way to parts of Oklahoma and the Dakotas. Avalanches of debris and hot ash that came out of the mountain killed 57 people. Rivers flooded around the mountain, trees were knocked over, and several feet of ash covered places around the mountain's base.

Mount Saint Helens' explosion created a vast land where there were no trees and no plant life. The mountain's peak looked completely different afterward. It is an incredible demonstration of the power of volcanoes and the geothermal workings of our planet.

When geothermal energy heats water, the result is called **hydrothermal circulation**. It's available at the earth's crust in different ways:

* **Geysers** are the most dramatic example. They're only found in a few places around the world—In Yellowstone National Park in Wyoming, and in Indonesia, Iceland, and New Zealand. Two-thirds of the world's geysers are found in Yellowstone Park. Geysers are unusual because it takes a special combination of factors to make one. **Magma** has to be near the surface of the earth. There also has to be a natural, underground plumbing system with tubes that create an outlet to the surface. When the water heats to a certain point and evaporates, the pressure of that steam and extremely hot water forces the water to shoot through the tubes to the surface of the earth. It can erupt a hundred feet high or more.

* **Hot springs** occur when water that's been heated deep underground seeps to the surface. For centuries, people have flocked to soak in hot springs, believing they had healing properties. The water can be heated by contact with magma, or it can be heated by contact with very hot rocks underground. You have to be careful about touching the water in hot springs—keep in mind some of them are heated by the same stuff that erupts out of volcanoes! The water can be boiling.

Words to Know

molten: melted by heat to form a liquid.

geothermal energy: heat energy that comes from the earth.

lava: molten rock that comes out of a volcano.

hydrothermal circulation: when water is heated by underground sources and rises to the surface.

geyser: a hot spring under pressure that shoots boiling water into the air.

magma: molten rock in the earth's crust.

hot springs: water that's superheated underground and comes to the surface of the earth.

Did you know?

The time it takes rainwater to soak through the ground before shooting out a geyser can be up to 500 years!

✳ **Mud pots** are hot springs that have a lot of dirt in them, so they're basically boiling mud. The mud bubbles away, just like hot water—but it's a lot messier.

✳ **Fumaroles** are vents or openings in the ground where the heated water underground comes out as steam instead of as a liquid. Fumaroles can give off gases, too, that are released by the hot rocks and magma.

Did you know?

In 1864, a hotel in Oregon was built that heated rooms using geothermal energy from underground hot springs.

The good news about hydrothermal circulation is that it's a renewable energy source. It all starts with rainwater that soaks through the earth's surface and seeps through the rocks below to access the heat deep in the ground. The water cycle will continue to replenish anything we use to convert that heat energy into electricity.

YOU'RE IN HOT WATER NOW!

People have used hydrothermal energy throughout history. The ancient Romans and early people of Iceland used it to heat their baths. The Romans even ran water through their walls to heat their homes and their swimming pools.

Today's geothermal power plants use the energy from water heated by the earth to generate electricity. The first thing they need to do is access that water. That means drilling deep into the earth. Then pipes bring that water or steam up to the power plant. The steam itself can directly run the turbines in the power plants.

CONDENSER

ELECTRICITY

DRY STEAM

GENERATOR

TURBINE

PRODUCTION WELL
DRY STEAM

INJECTION WELL
WATER

EARTH

Did you know?

Hot water pumped from below the earth's surface is used to heat almost all of the buildings in the capital of Iceland.

If the plant is using hot water, the air pressure over the water can be lowered, which helps create steam. If the water isn't hot enough to form steam, the plant can use that water to heat a liquid that boils easier than water. Different liquids begin to boil at different temperatures. Some liquids convert into steam at much lower temperatures than water. That can mean a temperature just above room temperature! The liquid turns into steam that powers the turbines.

There are several different kinds of geothermal power plants, which all use different ways to convert geothermal heat to power.

* **Dry steam:** In this type of system, the plant uses steam directly from underground. The steam turns a turbine that drives a generator. There's no need to burn fossil fuels to heat the steam because it's already heated underground. The first dry steam power plant was built in Italy in 1904.

* **Flash steam:** This kind of plant uses hot hydrothermal fluids that are rapidly dropped in pressure. They "flash," or turn into steam very quickly. The steam turns a turbine, and the turbine drives a generator. With this system, any remaining fluid can be vaporized again to get a little more energy.

* **Binary.** This type of power plant uses a second kind of liquid (called a "binary" liquid) that boils faster than water. The geothermal fluid is used to warm that second liquid.

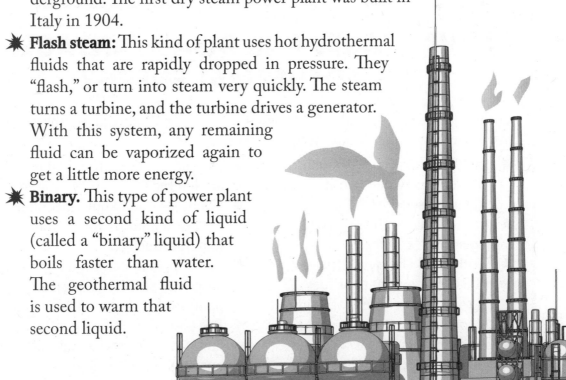

PUMP IT UP!

If you've ever been in a cave, you know that the temperature underground feels cooler in the summer and warmer in the winter than the air above ground. That's because the ground underneath the surface of the earth—even just a few feet—is usually at a constant temperature, between 50 and 60 degrees.

Did you know?

The United States uses more geothermal energy than any other country in the world.

Geothermal heat pumps take advantage of this steady temperature and tap into it as a way to heat and cool homes. This system works as a pump, circulating warmer and cooler air to where it's needed. Tubes extend in a geothermal system from a home deep into the ground. The tubes are filled with a coolant that can transport heat back and forth through a pump that controls whether the home needs heating and cooling. If it needs heat, the heated fluid returns up from underground. In the summer, the warmer air in the house gets pumped away, back down through the tubing to be cooled.

ADVANTAGES AND DISADVANTAGES OF GEOTHERMAL ENERGY

Geothermal energy is gentle on the environment, with many advantages:

* Usually little or no harmful gases are produced when geothermal energy is used.
* It is a relatively cheap way to generate electricity.
* Geothermal energy is efficient. It takes less amounts of fuel (in this case, geothermal fluids) to power more homes.
* Geothermal energy is a renewable energy source.

But some drawbacks of geothermal energy are:

* The sources of geothermal power are limited.
* Scientists don't know the impact of taking a lot of water from underground.
* Sometimes underground gases can stink and cause air pollution.
* The cost of installing geothermal pump systems for homes and businesses can be high.

MOLTEN LAVA CUPCAKES

Make Your Own

supplies

- oven
- 2 small bowls
- 1 large bowl
- ¾ cup chocolate chips
- ½ cup butter
- ¼ cup white chocolate chips
- 3 eggs
- electric mixer
- packaged brownie mix
- greased muffin tin
- raspberry jam

1. Preheat the oven to 400 degrees Fahrenheit. Combine the chocolate chips (not the white ones yet) and ¼ cup of the butter in a bowl. Melt them in the microwave, stirring to make sure it doesn't burn. Set aside.

2. Combine the white chocolate chips with the remaining butter and melt them in the microwave in the same way.

3. In a large bowl, beat the eggs with an electric mixer at high speed until they're doubled in size, about 5 minutes.

4. Gradually add the brownie mix to the eggs. Stir until it's very well blended. Gently stir in the melted chocolate (hold off on the white chocolate for now!).

5. Pour the batter into the muffin cups. Fill about half full. Put a little scoop of raspberry jam on top of each one. Top with some melted white chocolate.

6. Bake for about 12 minutes until the edges are set. The middles will still be soft.

7. Serve warm. When you break them open, the raspberry "lava" will come oozing out.

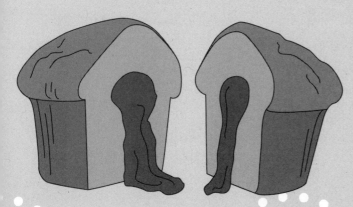

STEAMBOAT

Steam as power uses water as its fuel, combined with heat as an energy source. Here's how to make a very simple steamboat that will power itself across a small body of water. **Be sure to have an adult's help with this project, because you'll be using an open flame.**

supplies

- plastic milk container (a water bottle will be too soft)
- scissors
- thin copper tubing, 1/8-inch thick and 1 foot long
- wooden spoon
- small nail and hammer
- small tea candle
- body of water such as a bathtub

1. Cut the bottle in half, lengthwise. This will be the body of your boat.

2. Find the center of the copper tubing, and using the wooden spoon, curl the copper tubing around the handle to make a single coil right in the middle. The ends of the copper tubing should be parallel to each other when you're done and about an inch apart. Take the coil off of the spoon.

3. Using the small nail, carefully poke two holes in the back of the boat, about an inch apart. This is the part that used to be the bottom of the container. Make the holes about halfway up the back. Don't make the holes larger than the copper tubing, or else water will get into your boat. Push the two ends of the copper tubing through the holes, so that the coil is inside the boat and the ends stick out the back.

4. Set the tea candle into the body of your boat, directly underneath the coil. Depending on the placement of your holes, you may need to adjust the copper tubing a little by bending it up slightly so that the coil is over the candle. The two ends of the tubing should be low enough that they'll be under water.

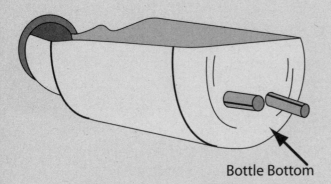

Bottle Bottom

5. Your boat is complete! To test it, fill up the bathtub. Suck gently on one end of the copper tubing to start water flowing into the tube.

6. Be sure the ends of your tubes are underwater the whole time, and light your candle.

7. When the water in the tube heats up, it'll turn to steam. The steam expands, pushing water out of the tubes and moving your boat. As the steam continues to expand, it hits water in the rest of the tube. Since that part of the tube is cold, the steam turns back into water, forming a vacuum in the tube. That pulls more water into the tube, which heats up and forms steam, and so on. The water being pushed and pulled into the tube gives your boat its motion.

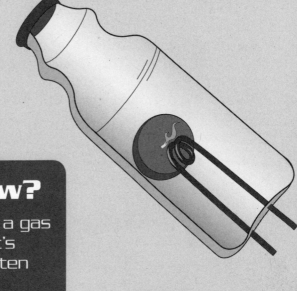

Did you know?

Some fumaroles give off a gas called sulfur dioxide. That's a gas that smells like rotten eggs!

FUMAROLE

You can create a fumarole right in your own kitchen. Experiment with several at a time to see what happens when more than one fumarole is present in a location. **You'll need an adult to help with this activity.**

supplies

- hammer and nail
- aluminum pie pan
- large pot with raised sides
- water
- stove
- oven mitts

1. Using the hammer and nail, poke a hole in the middle of the pie pan.

2. Fill the large pot halfway with water and set it on the stove on high heat.

3. When the water begins to steam, put the oven mitts on and set the pie plate upside-down on top of the pot. BE SURE TO STAND AWAY FROM THE POT. The steam will come shooting out of the hole. This is your fumarole!

4. Lift the pie plate off the pot by lifting the side farthest from you first. That way, the steam will escape out the back side, toward the back of the stove, not toward you. You'll have the pie plate in front of you like a shield.

5. Poke another hole in the pie plate and return it to the top of the pot. What happens? Keep poking holes and see what happens as you add fumaroles. The more holes there are to distribute steam, the less powerful each becomes.

Chapter 12

Biomass

The sun is our universe's big battery—generating power for everything on our planet. Plants use the sun's energy to grow and make food. When animals eat those plants, the plants pass along that energy to the animals. When the plants and animals die, that energy is still stored within their bodies. This **organic** material, which can be used as fuel, is called **biomass**. "Biomass" is short for **biological** mass.

Today, biomass comes mostly from plants, although some biomass comes from animal waste. In the past, oils harvested from whales were used as fuel, to light lamps.

Biomass can be converted to a fuel that is a substitute for gasoline in cars, for example. Besides fueling our cars, biomass can be burned to create other forms of energy like heat and light.

What's the difference between fossil fuels and biomass? Both come from dead plants and animals, right? The difference is that fossil fuels were made a long time ago, from plants and animals that died millions of years ago. Biomass uses organic material that was living very recently. Even though they both come from biological material, fossil fuels aren't considered biomass because the plants and animals that they come from died so long ago. The sources of fossil fuels are limited and not renewable.

Did you know?

Biomass fuels provide about 3 percent of the energy used in the United States.

Globally, biofuels are most commonly used to power vehicles, heat homes, and fuel cooking stoves. Biofuel industries are expanding in Europe, Asia, and the Americas.

Biomass is renewable because plants are always growing. The key is to strike a balance between how much biomass we use and how much we replant to keep new plants constantly growing. We need to grow more than we use.

HOW IT ALL STARTS

Plants get their energy from the sun. In a process called **photosynthesis**, plants combine the sun's light energy with water and **carbon dioxide** collected from the air. The plant uses that chemical energy for food to grow. And when humans and other animals eat plants, that chemical energy is passed on to them. When plants die, some of that energy still remains. If the plant rots or is burned, that energy is released. There are several types of biomass.

Wood. One of the first fuels ever used by humans, people all over the world still use wood as a fuel today. Wood from trees and other plants like shrubs is an easy source of energy. But not all wood is the same. Hardwood, for example,

Biomass is a renewable energy source.

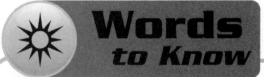

Words to Know

organic: something that is or was living.

biomass: biological material that can be used as fuel or as an energy source.

biological: having to do with something that is or was living.

photosynthesis: the process of plants using water and the sun's energy to grow.

carbon dioxide: a greenhouse gas made from burning something containing carbon.

bog: wet, spongy ground.

manure: animal waste.

burns longer than softwood and creates less smoke. Hardwood comes from broad-leafed trees like oak or maple trees. Softwood comes from conifers like pine trees.

Even wood scraps can be used as fuel. Wood waste condensed into wood "pellets" is used in pellet stoves, a cheap alternative to whole wood. The benefit of a pellet stove is that it burns very efficiently, so there is little carbon dioxide given off.

Peat. Made from partly decayed plants that grow in **bogs** or marshlands, even early Romans used peat as a fuel for their homes. Peat is a mossy, dense layer that's formed when plants can't completely decay in the wet, marshy conditions. If peat was left undisturbed for millions of years, it would eventually turn into coal.

To use peat, the water is forced out by applying pressure. After it's dry it can be burned as a fuel. There are areas where there aren't many trees, like Scotland and Ireland, that have used peat as the primary source of fuel for heat and cooking for thousands of years.

Manure. Wait—cow poo for energy? That's right. Livestock **manure** can be used to generate energy. For centuries, dried manure from animals like cows, camels, and even buffalo has been burned for heat and light. If it's dry enough, it can be burned directly, since much of the content is undigested plant material. Manure is still being used in some cultures as a source of heat energy. In India, cow dung is used, and in some desert regions camel manure is burned because of the lack of trees for wood.

Damp manure is high in methane. Methane is a greenhouse gas, but it's also a good source of energy. Scientists have figured out how to capture this gas from manure. It can be used right at the farm for electricity. In Michigan, there's a turkey farm that's using turkey manure to generate electricity for the farm's use. In Washington, a new facility will convert manure from local dairy farms into electricity for residences.

Garbage. Another unlikely source of energy is our own garbage! Trash like food scraps and paper can be used to generate energy. The waste can be burned to generate energy, or it can be "digested." To be digested, all the trash goes into a big tank. The methane gas that's formed as it rots is separated out from any remaining solids.

BIOFUEL

Biomass can be used for more than heat and light energy. It can also be used to fuel our cars. **Biofuel** is a fuel for vehicles that's made from organic material, instead of from fossil fuels. In some cases, vehicles use a "blend," which is biofuel mixed with fossil fuel–based gasoline. There are different kinds of biomass fuels:

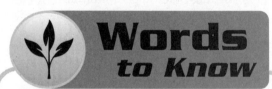

Words to Know

biofuel: fuel made from organic materials.

fermenting: the process of breaking down an organic substance.

methane: an odorless gas that is the main ingredient in natural gas.

biodiesel: fuel made from vegetable oils.

methanol: a type of alcohol.

catalyst: something that creates a chemical reaction in other substances.

* **Ethanol** is made when tiny organisms feed off the sugars made by plants like corn, sugar cane, and sugar beet. The organisms convert those sugars into ethanol, which is a flammable kind of alcohol that can run cars. Biofuel is mainly made by this **fermenting** process. Even yard clippings can produce ethanol.
* As plants decay, the decomposing material gives off **methane**, a gas that can be used as fuel.
* **Biodiesel** is made when crops like linseed, soybean, and rapeseed are processed for their oils. It can also be made from recycled restaurant grease. That's why some cars running on **biodiesel** smell like french fries!

Biodiesel can be used alone, or blended with traditional, petroleum-based fuels. Even if biodiesel is mixed with regular gasoline or diesel, it still means we're us-ing less fossil fuels than those vehicles would by running only on fossil fuels.

Where does the vegetable oil come from? It can be made from plant oil—or it can come straight from restau-rant waste! To make biodiesel, the oil is mixed with **methanol**, which is a kind of alcohol. Then, a **catalyst** like sodium hydroxide (a chemical) is put into the mixture. The chemical reaction creates the product known as biodiesel, with a little bit of waste product called glycerin. Glycerin can be used to make things like soap.

Did you know?

One cow's manure can produce enough energy to burn a 100-watt light bulb for an entire day!

THE ADVANTAGES AND DISADVANTAGES OF BIOMASS

Like all other energy sources, biomass has its benefits and its downfalls.

Some of the advantages of biomass are:

- 🍁 It's renewable. As long as we plant new sources faster than we harvest, biomass will always be around.
- 🍁 It's available all over the world, not just in one particular place on Earth.
- 🍁 Biomass creates relatively cheap fuel.
- 🍁 Using biomass is a good way of re-cycling. It can help eliminate some of the waste products (animal poo!) from big farms—waste that can cause pollution to air, land, and streams.

Disadvantages are:

- 🍁 Because living things are made of carbon, burning biomass still releases carbon dioxide into the environment. So biomass still contributes to our greenhouse gas problem.
- 🍁 Using land to grow crops for fuel could compete with the need for land to grow food.
- 🍁 There's still energy being used to both grow and harvest the biomass, so it's not entirely "free."

Make Your Own

FIRE STARTERS

If you're camping or if you want to start a fire in the fireplace, these easy fire starters do two things: They get the fire started easily and also recycle stuff from around the house. **Have an adult help you with melting and pouring the wax.**

supplies

- dryer lint
- cardboard egg carton (not Styrofoam)
- heavy pot
- water
- stove
- paraffin wax
- large metal or glass bowl
- oven mitts
- newspaper
- old towels or rags
- scissors

1. If you put a container near the dryer, any time anyone empties the lint catcher they can just pop the lint in the "lint saver." Then when you're ready to make the fire starters, you'll have a ready supply of lint.

2. Stuff as much dryer lint as you can into each compartment in the egg carton.

3. Fill the pot halfway with water and set it on the stove.

4. Cut the paraffin into small blocks and place it in the bowl. Set the bowl on top of the pot like a double boiler.

5. Slowly melt the paraffin by heating the water in the pot over low heat. Be very careful—you don't want to overheat the wax, since it is flammable. Also, use oven mitts to lift the bowl off once it's melted so you don't burn your hands.

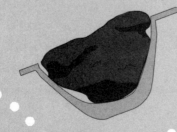

6. Spread newspaper out on your work surface. Then put towels or rags on the newspaper. Place the egg carton on top of the towels or rags. This is just to catch any drips or seepage from the egg carton. You may even want to do this step outside in case there's a spill.

7. Very carefully pour the melted wax into each of the egg carton containers, right over the dryer lint. The egg carton will absorb the wax very quickly, but don't worry. Fill each cup close to the top.

8. Cool until the wax becomes hard. It will take a couple of hours until it's really firm.

9. When the wax is hardened, use scissors to cut each of the cups apart into individual fire starters.

10. To start the fire, place one of the fire starters at each end of your stack of wood logs. Have an adult light them. They'll light very easily and the initial burn will catch your kindling on fire. All you need now are some marshmallows to roast!

Make Your Own

COW PIES

Here's a delicious way to remember that energy comes from all kinds of unlikely sources. Make up a batch of these edible "cow pies" and you've got a creative way to tell your friends and family all about alternative energy sources.

supplies

- 2 cups milk chocolate or semisweet chocolate chips
- 1 tablespoon of shortening
- bowl
- microwave
- up to 1 cup of mix-ins: try raisins, almonds, or crispy cereal
- spoon
- waxed paper
- candy corn
- refrigerator
- shredded coconut
- plastic baggie
- green food coloring

1. Melt the chocolate chips and shortening together in a bowl in the microwave. Keep checking and stirring—you don't want to burn your cow pies before they're even made. The mixture should be very smooth. Stir in your mix-ins.

2. Using a spoon, drop the mixture into circular piles on the waxed paper. Gently press a couple of candy corns into each. Let the candy harden in the refrigerator for a couple of hours.

3. Put the coconut in a plastic baggie. Squirt in a few drops of food coloring, and shake it well until the color is mixed through. Shake this coconut "grass" out onto plates and set the cow pies on top. Share with your friends and family!

PHOTOSYNTHESIS EXPERIMENT

Make Your Own

Biomass starts with plants. Even manure is biomass, because cows have to eat plants. The energy in plants comes from the sun. As they live and grow, plants use photosynthesis to convert light energy to chemical energy. With this experiment, you can see what happens if the plants don't have access to light energy.

supplies

- house plant with wide leaves (or you can use a tree, but make sure it's in direct sunlight)
- small pieces of paper
- scissors
- paper clips

1 Cut small pieces from the paper into shapes. Make the shapes smaller than the plant leaf, but large enough that they'll cover about half of the surface of the leaf.

2 Using the paper clips, carefully attach the shapes to a couple of the plant's leaves. Position the plant near a well-lit window.

3 After about four days, return to the plant and remove the paper shapes. What happened to the leaves? Your plant's leaves look the way they do because you blocked the light from reaching that part of the leaf. The plant couldn't perform photosynthesis for that section of the leaf. Without light, no chemical reaction could occur, and the plant wouldn't be able to live or grow. Without plants, biomass wouldn't be an option for energy.

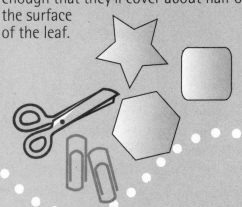

Chapter 13

The Future of Energy

It's things like the combustion engine in cars and trucks and all the electronics we use that drive our need for fossil fuels. As we've used more and more computers, video games, and televisions, and driven more cars more often, we've also used up almost all of the fossil fuels on the planet. There isn't very much oil and natural gas left. When we run out of fossil fuels, we will need alternative energy sources to power our lives.

It's probably a good idea to have these alternatives ready before we run out of fossil fuels, don't you think? Renewable sources, like solar, wind, and water, are options we're going to have to use more.

Swapping gas-powered vehicles for solar or hydrogen-powered ones, or finding better ways to generate electricity without burning coal are things that scientists all over the world are working on.

Energy really is a worldwide issue, so scientists are teaming up to find solutions. Not only do they need to identify sources of energy, but they have to figure out how to use them. And this part is really important. They have to come up with a way to do this **economically**, so we can afford it.

ENERGY AND THE ECONOMY

Energy use and the **economy** are tied together. For a hundred years up until 1985, our energy use increased as our economy grew. Our factories and industries used more and more energy to produce more and more cars, toys, and all the other things we use every day.

Since 1985 our energy use hasn't grown as quickly as our economy. That might be because so many of our factories have moved to other countries. We might not be making your T-shirt here in the United States. But the T-shirt factory in the Philippines uses energy—as well as the energy to get the T-shirt to the store in your town. The energy is still being used to make the things we buy. The challenge for the future is how we can build a strong **global economy** using less energy.

Another thing to think about: the machines that drill for oil use oil as their energy source. If we use one barrel of oil to drill for oil, how many barrels will we get? In the 1930s we got 100 barrels of oil for every one barrel we invested. Those were the days of big oil fields gushing easy oil. By the year 2000 we

Words to Know

economically: within a budget, cheaply.

economy: a system of producing and consuming goods and services.

global economy: refers to the economies of countries around the world being tied together, trading with each other and depending on each other.

were only getting 10 or 15 barrels for every barrel we used. That's because most of the oil that's left is harder to collect. It's easy to see that soon it will take an entire barrel of oil just to get one barrel of oil. Future energy sources need to give us lots and lots of energy for a small amount of energy used to produce it.

TAPPING INTO THE ENERGY

Transporting energy is another problem that needs to be solved. After the energy is generated or the source has been tapped, how will that energy travel to your house so you can use your toaster in the morning?

Did you know?

You can help by reducing the amount of energy you and your family need. That will save some of the current resources.

Things like coal and petroleum can be shipped by boat, train, and truck. You've seen how a solid like coal can be turned into a liquid "slurry" and sent along a pipeline. Natural gas and oil can also travel via pipeline. But you've also seen how those methods can have their share of problems—like oil spills.

Storing energy is another thing scientists have to consider when thinking about potential energy sources. Batteries can store energy, but they're expensive. Hydrogen is a good option, but because it's so light, it can easily leak through most containers. That makes hydrogen tough to store.

We need to have economical alternative energy sources before we run out of fossil fuels.

ENERGY CONSERVATION

Besides coming up with new ways to tap into energy sources or produce and use renewable energy sources, we need to **conserve** the energy resources we currently have. If you're thinking back to the first chapter where you saw that energy can't be created or destroyed, you may be wondering why we need to conserve energy if we can't destroy it. Good question.

Energy conservation is about using the minimum amount that you need. That way, our fossil fuels will last longer. And not only will saving energy help reduce the impact on the world's resources—using less energy will save us money, too. It just make sense not to be wasteful.

One of the biggest and most expensive uses of energy is for heating and cooling our homes. If you didn't have heat and air conditioning, the inside temperature of your house would be close to the temperature of the outdoors. On plenty of days—like beautiful days in the spring and fall—that doesn't sound so bad. But many days, it's far more comfortable to be able to set the temperature indoors to one that feels good to us. And that means using energy to heat or cool the inside of the house.

Did you know?

Although the United States has 5 percent of the world's entire population, it uses 23 percent of the world's energy.

One way to help minimize how much heating and cooling your house needs is to be sure it's properly insulated. That means it has a protective cushion that helps maintain a decent indoor temperature—keeping heat in during the winter and out during the summer. Can you think of other ways you can use less energy to stay warm or cool in your house?

The other big use of energy is transportation. Driving the family car not only uses fossil fuels, but it also belches out greenhouse gases.

These gases contribute to the amount of dangerous **ozone** that is accumulating in the air that we breathe, causing health problems and trapping heat in the earth's atmosphere. Reducing the amount of driving we do is one obvious way to cut down on energy consumption and protect the environment. How else can you get around?

THINK OF THE POSSIBILITIES

Coming up with alternative power sources takes some creative thinking. Although wind and solar power look especially promising as future sources of **sustainable** energy, scientists aren't just settling on those answers. They're looking for other alternatives, as well.

Words to Know

conserve: save or protect something.

ozone: a gas in the upper atmosphere that forms a layer around the planet called the ozone layer. The ozone layer protects the planet from the sun's most damaging rays and helps keep the planet a comfortable temperature. Ozone is a pollutant in the lower atmosphere.

sustainable: a resource that cannot be used up.

A man in Florida discovered that if he bombarded salt water with radio waves, he could separate hydrogen from the water. He could basically "burn" salt water!

A company in India developed a car that runs on compressed air. It's a concept similar to shooting torpedoes. The car uses air packed at high pressure to drive the pistons on the engine.

Other ideas that didn't quite fly have included making fuel from beer, grass, and sawdust! Crazy as these ideas sound, they're the first step in finding a solution—using creativity to brainstorm different possibilities.

TAKING CHARGE

Some people aren't waiting for the scientists to come up with answers. They're finding alternative fuel options on their own.

A 16-year-old boy in Virginia makes biodiesel fuel in his basement from cooking oil. His family has saved money on traditional gasoline, helped the environment (the exhaust is clean), and he's reusing a waste product (the used cooking oil). The only drawback? Because the oil he uses has been recycled from restaurants, the exhaust does smell like french fries sometimes.

In Vermont, a small electrical company captures the methane gas from rotting garbage in a large landfill. Then it burns the methane gas to generate enough electricity to power 2,600 homes. In fact, across the country there are hundreds of landfills generating electricity in the same way.

A Swiss schoolteacher spent a year and a half driving around the world in a solar-powered car. Once it's charged, the car can travel up to 200 miles before needing to be recharged. His mission was to bring attention to the possibilities for sustainable energy in cars.

Who knows what people will come up with to power our world? It's a task for everyone to figure out—even you can help find an answer. Maybe you're the one who will tap your creativity and invent a new source of energy, or a way to conserve it. It's a global issue, which means we're all responsible for seeking solutions. The answers are out there—it will just take some brain energy to uncover them.

SOLAR-POWERED VEHICLE

HOME ENERGY AUDIT

Make Your Own

How energy efficient is your home? You can find out by giving your home a once-over with this home energy audit. When you see where your home is losing energy then you can do something about it.

supplies

- compass
- pad of paper
- pen
- piece of plastic wrap about 5 inches wide
- pencil
- tape
- thermometer (or 2, if you have them)
- work gloves
- ruler

Room	Score
Overall	20
Drafts	10
—windows	5
—doors	10
Temps	
Wood burning fireplace	4
Basement	10
Attic	30
House Temp	6
Night winter temp.	10
Summer / air conditioner temp.	5
Water heater temp.	10

Total ✗ 120

1. To begin your home energy audit, stand in front of your home holding the compass. Which direction do most of your home's windows face? The direction determines how much the weather has an impact on your heating and cooling. For example, rooms that have lots of windows facing east and west may get the full heating impact of the sun as it travels through the sky. You may be cooling these rooms more.

While you can't change the position of your house, you can close the shades when it's hot out to help cool down the rooms that are warmed by the sun.

If your house is exposed to the north, called a northern exposure, you may find it's very cold in the winter when northern winds blow cold air against it. Trees planted along the northern side of the house can help shield it from the cold winds.

2. Now take your pad and pen and make a chart. Put "Room" at the top of one column and "Score" at the top of the next.

Make Your Own HOME ENERGY

3. Begin the scoring by assessing the overall condition of your house. If you live in an area that gets cold—below 30 degrees Fahrenheit—check to see if you have storm windows and doors. (You may have to ask your parents about whether you have storm windows or doors.) If you do, give your house 20 points. If you don't, give your house zero points. Storm windows and doors are second windows and doors that you put on in the winter. They provide an extra layer of insulation against cold weather.

4. Make a note of how much insulation your house needs. You'll use this number later. If you live in the south or along the coast, your house needs about 7 to 9 inches of insulation. If you live between Pennsylvania and Colorado, you'll need about 8 to 10 inches of insulation. If your home is between Michigan and Idaho, you'll need about 9 to 11 inches. And if you're in the northern states, you'll need around 10 to 12 inches of insulation.

5. Take the piece of plastic wrap and tape it along the length of the pencil so it hangs down like a flag. This will detect any drafts in your rooms.

6. Start in your living room. A day with some wind is a good one for checking drafts. Hold your draft detector up to all of the windows and the doors. Go all the way around each one along where the cracks are. Watch carefully to see if there is any movement of the plastic wrap. If it moves at all, you've got a draft. On your scoring sheet, give yourself scores based on whether you've got any drafts: If there are any drafts, give your home a zero on your score sheet. If there are no drafts around your windows, give your home a 10 on your score sheet. And if there are no drafts around your doors, give your room a 5 on the score sheet. It's more likely that you'll have drafts around your windows than your doors, so that's why there's a difference in the scoring. Check for drafts in your whole house.

AUDIT

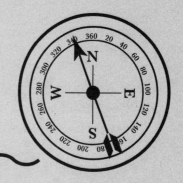

7. Now test your home's exterior wall insulation. Tape a thermometer along an outside wall. This is a wall with a window or outside door on it. Take a reading after several hours. Then place the thermometer in the center of the same room. Try to keep the thermometer at about the same height as it was on the outside wall. Leave it alone and check it in a couple of hours. (If you have two thermometers, you can take the readings at the same time.) If the readings are about the same (under 5 degrees difference), give your room the score of 10. If the difference is more than 5 degrees, give your room a score of zero.

8. Add 4 points to your score if you don't have a wood-burning fireplace. If you do have one, but the damper is always closed when you're not using the fireplace, add 4. But if the damper is always open, give your house a zero. Heat can easily escape out of the open fireplace up the chimney when the damper is open!

9. If you have a basement and it's heated, give your house 10 points. If you don't have a basement but the floor under your home is insulated, score a 10, too. But if there's no insulation or an unheated basement, give your house a zero.

10. Now check your attic. Wearing the work gloves and using the ruler, measure the depth of the insulation on the ceiling. Compare this measurement to the number you figured out in step four. If you're within the recommended thickness of insulation (or you've got more than recommended), give your house a score of 30. If it's less than 2 inches under the recommended amount, score a 25. If the insulation is 4 inches under the recommended amount, score a 15. If the amount is 6 inches less, give your house a 5. And if there's less than 2 inches total, give your house a score of zero.

ISULATION

HOME ENERGY AUDIT

11. Now think about your family's overall energy use. If your family keeps the temperature at 68 degrees Fahrenheit or less during the day in the winter, give your house a score of 6. For each degree over 68 that the thermostat is set, take away an extra point. And if it's over 70? Zero points.

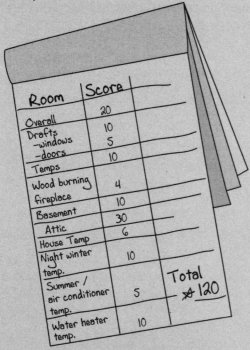

Room	Score
Overall	20
Drafts	10
–windows	5
–doors	10
Temps	
Wood burning fireplace	4
Basement	10
Attic	30
House Temp	6
Night winter temp.	10
Summer / air conditioner temp.	5
Water heater temp.	10
Total	120

12. Now think about the temperature in the house in the winter at night. If you keep it set at 60 degrees Fahrenheit or under, score 10 points. Take away one point for each degree it's set over 60. And if it's 66 or above? Score zero.

13. Think about the summer now. If you don't have air conditioning, score 7. If you do have it, and the temperature is set at or above 78 degrees, give your house the score of 5. Take away one point for every degree the temperature is set under 78. And if it's set below 76, score zero.

14. Finally, check the temperature on your water heater. If the temperature is under 120 degrees Fahrenheit, give your house the score of 10. If it's between 120 and 140, give your house the score of 5. If it's over 140, your house earns zero points.

15. To make the final assessment of your home energy audit, add together the scores. If the total is less than 100, your home isn't doing too well in the energy conservation department. Use what you learned while doing the audit to figure out ways your family can make adjustments. You can save energy and money!

Glossary

AC electricity: alternating current, where the electrons flow in one direction, then the other. AC can travel over long distances.

amps: measure the electrical current, or the amount of electrons flowing per second.

anemometer: an instrument used to measure the wind. The number of times it spins is calculated and converted into miles per hour.

anode: where electrons are separated from hydrogen in a fuel cell.

atmosphere: the gases that surround the earth.

atom: the smallest particles that make everything.

biodiesel: fuel made from vegetable oils.

biofuel: fuel made from organic materials.

biological: having to do with something that is or was living.

biomass: biological material that can be used as fuel or as an energy source.

bog: wet, spongy ground of rotting vegetation.

butane: a flammable gas found in petroleum and natural gas.

carbon dioxide: a greenhouse gas made from burning something containing carbon.

carbon monoxide: a greenhouse gas produced by burning fossil fuels.

catalyst: something that creates a chemical reaction in other substances.

cathode: where the electrons return from the circuit in a fuel cell.

cell: the small units of a living thing.

chemical energy: energy produced by a chemical reaction.

chemical reaction: when atoms are rearranged in a substance to make a new substance.

circuit: a complete path of an electrical current.

coal: a non-renewable fossil fuel burned to generate electricity.

combustible: something that can catch on fire and burn easily.

combustion engine: a heat engine that burns fuel.

compressed: pressed together very tightly, so something takes up less space.

condense: when water or another liquid cools down, it changes from a gas (water vapor) back into a liquid (water).

conduct: to transfer something.

conserve: save or protect something.

control rods: devices to absorb neutrons.

controlled chain reaction: when a nuclear reaction is controlled, allowing only one neutron to continue on from a split atom to hit a new atom.

crude oil: oil in its natural form, right out of the ground.

dam: a large, strong wall that holds back water.

DC electricity: direct current, where the electrons flow in just one direction. DC weakens over distances.

debris: the remains of something, such as dirt, rocks, and vegetation.

decay: when an atom breaks down.

drag: a force that slows down or resists the wind.

drill bit: the very hard tip of the drill that grinds through layers of rock.

economically: within a budget, cheaply.

economy: a system of producing and consuming goods and services.

electric charge: when there is an imbalance of electrons, either too many or not enough.

electricity: energy made available by the flow of an electric charge through a conductor.

electrolysis: the process used to capture hydrogen from water using electricity.

electrolyte: the membrane that controls the flow of protons.

electrons: the particles in atoms with a negative charge.

element: a very basic substance made of all the same atoms.

Glossary

energy: the ability or power to do things, to work.

energy audit: measuring how much energy is used and finding where it is being wasted.

energy carrier: something that can transfer energy to something else, like a lamp. Something that moves energy in a usable form from one place to another.

energy conservation: decreasing energy use.

energy source: something with stored energy that can be transformed into usable energy. Examples include oil, coal, natural gas, the sun, and the wind.

energy vampire: when something plugged in, like a toaster or a computer, uses some energy even when itís not on or being used.

environment: an area that includes plants and animals.

erosion: when land is worn away by water flow.

ethanol: alcohol made from plants used as fuel.

evaporate: when a liquid heats up and changes into a gas.

fermenting: the process of breaking down an organic substance.

fission: the nuclear reaction where a neutron splits an atom, releasing heat energy and more neutrons.

flammable: something that burns very easily.

force: physical pressure that's applied to something.

fossil fuels: non-renewable energy sources such as oil, natural gas, and coal. Made from plants and animals that died millions of years ago.

fuel cell: something that produces a steady stream of electricity.

fumarole: an opening in the ground where steam comes out.

fuse: to join together under high heat by melting.

generator: a machine that converts mechanical energy into electricity.

geothermal energy: renewable heat energy that comes from the earth.

geyser: a hot spring under pressure that shoots boiling water into the air.

global economy: refers to the economies of countries around the world being tied together, trading with each other and depending on each other.

global warming: the gradual warming of the planet.

gravity: the force of attraction that pulls all objects to the earth's surface.

greenhouse gases: gases like carbon monoxide and carbon dioxide that get into the atmosphere and trap heat.

hot springs: water that is superheated underground and comes to the surface of the earth.

hydraulic: using water to operate or move something.

hydroelectricity: electricity produced by water power.

hydrogen: the simplest and the most abundant element in the universe. Hydrogen can be used as an energy carrier.

hydropower: renewable power from water.

hydrothermal circulation: when water is heated by underground sources and rises to the surface.

irrigate: moving water from one area to another to water crops.

joule: a unit of electrical energy.

kinetic energy: energy in motion.

lava: molten rock that comes out of a volcano.

law of conservation of energy: the idea that energy cannot be created or destroyed, just transferred between objects.

Glossary

liquefied: when something is changed into a liquid form.

magma: molten rock in the earth's crust.

manure: animal waste.

mass: a collection of particles.

matter: the stuff that everything in the universe is made out of.

mechanical energy: energy that uses physical parts you can see, like the parts of a machine.

meltdown: an uncontrolled reaction in a nuclear power plant.

membrane: thin material that allows some materials to pass through but not others. In a fuel cell it allows protons to pass through.

meteorological: involving the weather and climate.

methane: a gas with no color or smell made from natural sources. The main ingredient in natural gas.

methanol: a type of alcohol.

miner: person who works in a mine.

moderator: a substance that slows the rate of a nuclear reaction in the power plant by keeping it cool.

molecule: a group of atoms bound together. Molecules combine to form matter.

molten: melted by heat to form a liquid.

mud pot: a hot spring with a lot of dirt in it—boiling mud.

natural gas: a non-renewable fossil fuel that is a common energy source for heat.

neutrons: the particles in the nucleus with no charge.

non-renewable: energy sources that can be used up, that we can't make more of.

nuclear: harnessing the power of atoms makes nuclear power an important source of energy.

nuclear fusion: the process of hydrogen converting to helium and releasing energy.

nuclear reactor: the place where a nuclear reaction takes place in a nuclear power plant.

nucleus: the center of an atom.

ohms: measures the amount of resistance to the electrical current, like how hard it is for the electricity to flow.

oil rig: a large drill that punctures the earth where oil is, making a hole that allows oil to be brought to the surface.

orbit: a repeating path that circles around something else.

organic: something that is or was living.

outcropping: piece of rock sticking up above the ground.

ozone: a gas in the upper atmosphere that forms a layer around the planet called the ozone layer. The ozone layer protects the planet from the sun's most damaging rays and helps keep the planet a comfortable temperature. Ozone is a pollutant in the lower atmosphere.

passive solar: solar heat that's created without equipment.

permeable: a substance that liquid (or gas) can flow through.

petroleum: non-renewable fossil fuel used to heat homes and fuel cars. Also called oil and gasoline.

photosynthesis: the process of plants using water and the sun's energy to grow.

photovoltaic cells: solar cells that transform solar energy into electricity.

pistons: sliding pieces that move up and down or back and forth.

potential energy: stored energy.

power: energy used over time.

power grid: the network of cables that transport electricity all over the country.

propane: a colorless gas found in natural gas and in crude oil. Often used in cooking.

Glossary

Proton Exchange Membrane (PEM): a compact fuel cell that can power cars. One fuel cell doesn't provide enough energy to run a car, so several PEMs are piled together into one unit called a stack.

protons: the particles in the nucleus with a positive electrical charge.

radiant energy: light

radiate: to spread outward.

radiation: when energy moves away from the source in waves.

refinery: factory where petroleum is separated into different oil types.

renewable: an energy source that can replenish itself.

repel: to resist or push away.

reservoir: a body of water that's stored for future energy use. It can be natural or man-made.

seismograph: an instrument that measures vibrations under the ground.

shaft: a tunnel or passage.

slurry: a mixture of coal and water, which allows coal to travel through pipelines.

solar: renewable energy from the sun that can be captured to heat water or generate electricity.

solar cells: devices used to capture the sun's radiant energy.

sorbent: a material that can absorb a liquid or semi-liquid.

static electricity: a build-up of an electric charge on an object (like you!)

stored energy: energy that is there, waiting to be used.

strip mining: the process of mining coal where the top layers of the earth are removed.

substance: matter.

substation: between the power plant and homes, where electricity is reduced in voltage.

sustainable: a resource that cannot be used up.

terminals: positive and negative contact points on a battery.

tide: the daily rising and falling of ocean water, based on the pull of the moon's and sun's gravity.

transformer: a device that changes the voltage of electricity.

turbine: a machine that turns when a force is applied to it, sending mechanical energy to a generator. Also a wind machine that converts wind power to electricity.

uncontrolled chain reaction: when the splitting of atoms and the release of energy and neutrons is magnified and grows rapidly.

uranium: the element used as fuel in nuclear reactions.

voltage: the amount of force in the electricity.

volts: electrical pressure. The more volts something has, the more intense or forceful it is.

water cycle: the endless process that water travels through on Earth. It evaporates to become water vapor in clouds. Then it condenses into liquid water in the form of rain or snow, over and over again.

water wheel: a large wheel with buckets or paddles that move as water flows through it.

watts: measures how much energy is being consumed by an electrical object.

wind farm: a group of wind machines that generate electricity from the wind.

wind: renewable energy that can be transformed into electricity.

work: any kind of activity.

x-ray: radiation that allows doctors to see your bones.

Resources

BOOKS

Challoner, Jack. *Eyewitness: Energy*. DK Children, 2000.

Fridell, Ron. *Earth-Friendly Energy*. Lerner Publications, 2008.

Gleason, Carrie. *Geothermal Energy: Using the Earth's Furnace*. Crabtree Publishing Company, 2008.

Green, Dan. *Why Matter Matters*. Kingfisher, 2008.

Hammond, Richard. *Can You Feel the Force?* DK Children, 2006.

Lafferty, Peter. *Eyewitness: Force and Motion*. DK Children, 1999.

Langwith, Jaqueline. *Renewable Energy*. Greenhaven Press, 2008.

Peppas, Lynn. *Ocean, Tidal and Wave Power: Power from the Sea*. Crabtree Publishing Company, 2007.

VanCleave, Janice. *Janice VanCleave's Energy for Every Kid*. Wiley, 2005.

Walker, Niki. *Biomass: Fueling Change*. Crabtree Publishing Company, 2007.

Walker, Niki. *Generating Wind Power*. Crabtree Publishing Company, 2007.

WEB SITES

www.eia.doe.gov/kids
Energy Information Administration's kid page
Some energy facts and timelines about different energy sources.

www.eere.energy.gov/kids
Energy Efficiency and Renewable Energy by the United States Department of Energy
Games and information about saving energy.

www.energyquest.ca.gov
Energy Quest from the California Energy Commission
Learn about energy conservation by playing this online game.

www.explorit.org/science/energy.html
Q & A from Explorit
A great list of questions and answers from a California science museum.

www.powerhousekids.com
Powerhouse Kids
Learn about gas and electrical energy.

www.fplsafetyworld.com
Florida Power and Light
Games and pages that explore energy.

www.energystar.gov/kids
Energy Star
Learn about ways you can help save the earth's energy resources.

Index

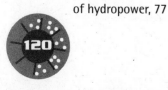

Index

Index